switch
OFF

switch
OFF

How to find **calm**
in a **noisy** world

Angela Lockwood

WILEY

First published in 2017 by John Wiley & Sons Australia, Ltd
42 McDougall St, Milton Qld 4064
Office also in Melbourne

Typeset in 11/15 pt ITC Garamond Std

© The Place for Health (STAM Media Pty Ltd) 2017

The moral rights of the author have been asserted

National Library of Australia Cataloguing-in-Publication data:

Creator:	Lockwood, Angela, author.
Title:	Switch Off: how to find calm in a noisy world / Angela Lockwood.
ISBN:	9780730336280 (pbk.)
	9780730336303 (ebook)
Notes:	Includes index.
Subjects:	Self-management (Psychology)
	Time management.
	Self-help techniques.
	Relaxation.
Dewey Number:	158.1

Cover design: Wiley
Cover image: © topform / Shutterstock
Advert image: Happyness Photography

Printed in Singapore by C.O.S. Printers Pte Ltd

10 9 8 7 6 5 4 3 2 1

Disclaimer
The material in this publication is of the nature of general comment only, and does not represent professional advice. It is not intended to provide specific guidance for particular circumstances and it should not be relied on as the basis for any decision to take action or not take action on any matter which it covers. Readers should obtain professional advice where appropriate, before making any such decision. To the maximum extent permitted by law, the author and publisher disclaim all responsibility and liability to any person, arising directly or indirectly from any person taking or not taking action based on the information in this publication.

Contents

ABOUT THE AUTHOR

Angela Lockwood is an occupational therapist whose boundless energy sees her equally at ease working with children as standing in front of a packed audience delivering a keynote. Through living life at full-speed, Angela has learned first-hand the power of 'switching off', allowing her to overcome seemingly impossible challenges and achieve success in life, love and career.

As a star hockey player during her school years, Angela had her sights set on the Sydney Olympics. However, after fracturing her skull during a game—an injury that would have stopped most in their tracks—her experiences learning to talk again and re-think her approach to life inspired her to change her path to occupational therapy, propelling her into a career that she was made for.

With a desire to help children have the best start in life, Angela is one of the most respected pediatric occupational therapists in Australia and abroad. Her knack for creating success has allowed her to become the go-to person for industries including government, schools, universities, hospitals, emergency services, health and wellbeing providers, banks, real estate institutes, not-for-profits and media outlets, and to fulfill roles such as CEO, keynote speaker, author, health and fitness instructor, trainer, motivator, mum and wife.

After the success of her first book *The Power of Conscious Choice*, a publication aimed at helping people to simplify the way they make decisions, she launched The Place for Health, an online hub that aims to educate health professionals and caregivers on how to prioritise their own mental and physical wellbeing. She also works with individuals and organsiations, hosts retreat events and conducts programs in schools to help people continue to live the life they choose with the energy needed to get them there.

Practicing as she preaches, Angela lives on the beautiful coastline of Northern New South Wales with her husband and two gorgeous children. She spends as much time as possible with her feet in the sand and takes the time to look up and around, forever thankful.

ACKNOWLEDGEMENTS

Many people have helped make this book happen. From Wiley, thank you to senior commissioning editor Lucy Raymond for seeing my vision and sharing my passion, to editor Jem Bates for your attention to detail, and to the whole Wiley team for your professionalism and for believing in me and the book.

To my husband Matt: with you beside me I can truly live the life I choose. And to my beautiful children: I hope you continue to embrace possibility, take the time to look around you and always be thankful for the gift of life.

To the tribe of friends who have supported me through this writing project: thank you for being there when I needed a helping hand.

Several people whom I deeply admire willingly shared their time and expertise with me, allowing me to channel a small part of it through this book. A big thank you to Shivani Gupta, Dr Jenny Brockis and Jenna Kennedy.

Lastly, I want to acknowledge the beautiful world that surrounds me. Inspiration was always in my reach through the crystal-blue ocean, the green forests, the birds that sat beside me on the verandah while I wrote—and the vibrant cafes where I sought to refuel! It is when we look up and around us that we realise we already have everything we need in life and more. We just need to slow down long enough to enjoy it.

INTRODUCTION
A MESSAGE FROM THE AUTHOR

Most people use business, self-help and motivational books as a feel-good tool. They read a few pages before falling asleep at night. They tell their friends about this book they are reading and the ideas it offers on how to get the most out of life. With thousands of these books published each year, we can be certain there are plenty of good titles out there, in print and online. Let's not make this one of those books that you dip into every now and again but that only gathers dust on the shelf when you're done. It would be such a wasted opportunity.

I wrote this book for one reason: there are too many good people who are doing everything they can in life but are finding themselves overwhelmed and exhausted by it all. I want to show those people how they can do whatever they want in life if they just *slow down*. The only way you are going to get any benefit from this book is if you read it slowly and thoughtfully. Not because it is especially content heavy, but to allow the messages to sink in and make a positive impact on your thinking and your actions. I don't want you to waste your time.

Switch Off interweaves stories, research, reflections, information and activities in ways that I hope will encourage you to take what you have learned and apply the strategies directly in your life. You will find more than 250 ideas on how to help you switch off, slow down and regain control, so now you really don't have any excuse not to take action.

I hope you will feel while reading that you have someone supporting you along the way, because you do. I understand how hard it is to try to maintain control over the hectic busyness of life, so let's not make it any more complicated than it needs to be, and you surely do not have to do it on your own.

I vividly recall the day I experienced my own panic attack. Or at least I think that was what it was; all I knew was whatever was happening to me felt scary and all-consuming. Early that morning I drove my husband to the train station to connect to his flight to the top of Australia, where he would be working for the next few months. After saying goodbye I drove off, holding in my tears, not wanting the kids to see how sad I was to see him go. I never have been one to cry.

I dropped the kids off at school and drove to a scheduled meeting with a consultant. I had been feeling she wasn't right for the business, but I hadn't had time to look for anyone else. After a long discussion on how important technical issues were yet to be resolved, she slid an invoice across the table, apologised for the size of the bill and promised to fix the unsettled problems the following month! I could feel my chest start to tighten, my breathing quicken and what felt like a vice clamping down on either side of my head. I was trying hard to hold it together, but my body was telling me I was about to explode. I stood up, thanked her for her time and walked out of the meeting half an hour early, leaving an unambiguous impression that I was not happy.

As I walked towards my car I felt like the Hulk at the moment of transformation, and then my phone rang. It was the printer of my first book, telling me the layout was wrong…and it was going to print in four days. My heart raced faster, I looked around wildly for an escape, not sure where to turn, but knowing I had to get out of whatever this crazy feeling was. I was on the brink.

I retreated to the safe familiarity of my car, closed the door, took a breath and a whirlwind of emotions overcame me. Basically I lost it. For the first time in my life I felt completely out of control…and alone in my chaos. I was swept up in one of the scariest feelings I have ever felt. I couldn't control my breathing, tears flooded down my cheeks, my hands trembled, my eyes were wide as plates. I just didn't know what to do. I froze in this scary moment.

With the clarity that only hindsight affords, I came to recognise the three things that had led me to this moment: I was overconnected, overwhelmed and completely overstimulated. Too many people were wanting too much from me (including myself). I was being crushed by an ever-growing to-do list, living in a state of hyper-arousal, persistently on the edge. Life at full throttle was too much, too full and too frantic. It was no longer working for me. I needed it to *stop*. One of my favourite mantras is 'you only get one shot at life'. I had interpreted this as meaning I must do everything and do it now. But it was taking its toll.

As soon as I called a friend I knew I was no longer alone. That frozen moment in the car marked a moment of choice: I could suck it up, take a big deep breath and keep going, or I could see it as a sign, a message, a wake-up call that it was time to make a change, to see things differently and more importantly to do things differently. I had been given an opportunity to take a step back from the chaos and slow down, and that's exactly what I did.

This life-changing experience (it really was) gave me an opportunity to find a calm place within the noise of my life. It forced me to stop and take notice, to reconnect with the side of me I had been suppressing in my wild pursuit of living life to the full, to re-examine what I wanted out of life. This wasn't going to happen through attending a retreat in India or seeking a meditation guru or taking a 90-day trek through the mountains. This, right here, right now, was my opportunity to find calm in the chaos.

Reading this book you will discover that my experience, my story, is not at all unique, that many people yearn for time on their own and for a less complicated life in which they feel in control, at least for a time. That is what this book is for. To help you to see that, rather than being a luxury, slowing down is a necessity, and that it may be the key to helping you live the life you choose.

Part I
The burden of connection

The background hum of the television was mostly drowned out by the whirr of the oven and the ruckus of the kids getting ready for dinner, until a prime-time television news report broke through the noise and caught my attention. A revolutionary new 'boot camp' had been started in South Korea to help kids as young as eight learn how to play with their peers and take time away from technology. In a first of its kind (other such initiatives have since followed), this residential program brought city kids into a natural setting where they got to run outside, build forts and generally mix with other kids—with no iPad, smartphone or television in sight. The idea was to teach children how to be children again, without technology.

I stood in the kitchen, a tea towel draped over my shoulder, riveted to the story. The screen showed boys aged around 9 to 13 standing in loose formation, bringing to mind a scene from *M*A*S*H*, the military comedy series from the 1970s. Except these were not recruits in army greens but young boys of every shape and size, most of them not looking at all pleased to be there. Their parents waved goodbye anxiously and drove off, leaving their sons in the hands, not of a stern-looking drill sergeant, but of a middle-aged couple who looked more like office workers than boot camp instructors.

But this was no typical boot camp. It was a camp for troubled youth whose main challenge was an addiction to technology that had impacted their behaviour, their learning and their friendships. At home they were forever sprawled in front of the television or glued to their computer, rudely refusing to do their homework and chores, isolating themselves from their peers. As the story progressed we saw the same young boys climbing trees, jumping into a creek, reading books. To me they looked like...kids, and they were. Except they had lost connection with the childhood joys associated with being outdoors, being creative and playing with real-life friends. Their problem was not simply playing too many computer games; it went deeper. The interviewer asked one young boy how he was finding the program. With eyes downcast and in a soft voice he replied, 'It's good, but I miss my computer...I didn't think I could live without it'.

As the curry bubbled on the stove behind me, I couldn't keep my eyes off the screen. During my career as an occupational therapist I have worked a lot with children with learning, behavioural and developmental challenges. I imagined (or hoped) what I was seeing here was a problem that applied to only a very small demographic of the global community. I knew South Korea was one of the world's most wired nations. But surely this was not a serious issue, big enough and prevalent enough that kids needed to be taken from their parents, forcibly disengaged from their technological devices in order for them to learn to be kids again. Well, it seems I had no idea. The problem for all of us is indeed bigger than I, or any of us, could have imagined, and it is not going away.

CHAPTER 1

Work–life integration

The challenge of being overconnected and unable to switch off from technology transcends age, race, education and geography, and it doesn't stop with technology. Many of us feel the effects of living life in the fast lane. Our frenetic pace, racing from one meeting to the next and one activity to the next, is affecting our ability to take time out, slow down, switch off and refuel. With our bodies and minds constantly 'switched on', our health and wellbeing are increasingly paying the price. We are in a state of chronic overconnection, overwhelm and overstimulation. This is a growing global problem.

Searching for slow

In 2004 Canadian journalist and best-selling author Carl Honoré published *In Praise of Slow*, in which he outlines the sociological and psychological implications of a speed-obsessed culture and warns of the potential negative consequences of our obsession with speed. Honoré traces the history of our relationship with time and asks, 'Why are we always in such a rush?' and 'When are we going to slow down?' Arguing that 'Evolution works on survival of the fittest, not the fastest,' he proposes an alternative way of thinking and living, which he calls 'the slow revolution'.

To achieve more we do not have to keep pushing ourselves to *do* more; in fact we are capable of achieving more through doing less. Most people reading this will want to jump immediately to the 'how to' section. It is a modern-day conundrum: how can we do more by doing less?

> To achieve more we do not have to keep pushing ourselves to *do* more; in fact we are capable of achieving more through doing less.

In Praise of Slow was written more than ten years ago. This way of thinking seemed then to be espoused only by hippies living in the mountains who were rarely in touch with the 'real world'. How times have changed! Roll forward ten years and it seems the slow revolution has started to find its way into the consciousness of people you would least expect to have time for it. Executives in boardrooms are searching for ways to integrate slow living into their fast-paced, demand-driven lives, and as suggested in the Korean news report, parents are embracing the slow revolution for their children.

We want to have it all—a fat pay packet, a successful business, prestige during the week, and the weekend spent stand-up paddle boarding, sipping lattes and coaching the soccer team. To have it all, though, we need to make some changes to how we are living. Back in 1948, in his best-seller *How to Stop Worrying and Start Living*, Dale Carnegie spoke of the importance of living a life free of worry about the constraints of time and other pressures. His message evidently remains compelling, as the book continues to be one of the most recommended business self-help books almost seventy years later.

If we have known for a long time, having been warned by such authoritative voices as these, that living life constantly 'switched on' is negatively affecting our physical and psychological wellbeing, then why haven't we taken notice?

Part of the answer lies in the context of the rapid pace of change in our world. The changes that have resulted from the growth in population, communications and technology over the past hundred years are quite astonishing. Here are some examples taken from the years my grandmother has been alive:

- As many people live in Sydney today as lived in the whole of Australia in 1915.

- Traditionally school children relied on paper and ink. Today's students learn using personal tablets, computers, interactive boards and live video linkups, starting as early as preschool.

- A handwritten letter to a friend could take weeks to get to London from Australia; now it takes milliseconds to send a message via instant messaging to the other side of the world.

- The most influential people were once politicians; now we look to business leaders, bloggers and celebrities for guidance.

- People would send a letter or walk to a friend's house for a cup of tea and a catch-up; now there are social media platforms with millions (sorry, billions) of users, allowing you to connect instantly with your friends (and with people you don't even know!) all over the world.

- According to the Australian Bureau of Statistics, in 1915 just 498 divorces were recorded in Australia; today's annual figure exceeds 47 000.

- Television, computers, phones, cars, air travel, the pop-up toaster, disposable nappies, ballpoint pens, batteries, aerosol cans, stereos and the internet, all now taken for granted in our society, were invented during the lifetime of my grandmother. It is mind-blowing to think that none of these things we so take for granted even existed when she was young. Now we cannot imagine life without them. (Think about the changes you might yet see in your own lifetime or 100 years from now.)

We cannot deny these changes have benefited us in so many ways. It is our ability to keep up with the *speed* of change that is taking its toll on our health and wellbeing. So why haven't we learned how to switch off when we need to? It comes down to two factors: expectations and priorities.

Life role evolution

Life roles evolve. If we roll back a few thousand years, the chief expectations of our early ancestors were to eat and to stay alive. Life was based on survival, so daily actions focused on finding adequate shelter, gathering enough food and making sure you were not eaten—with social roles distinguishing, for example, hunters from gatherers. Not complicated perhaps, but life had its risks and stressors, like being taken by a lion or dying of starvation.

Roll forward a few thousand years to the 19th century and expectations had changed significantly. By common practice men worked for pay to provide for their family while women were expected to run the household, raise children, and keep the family fed, clothes washed and needs satisfied. Days were spent working to provide a roof over the family's heads and put food on the table—not so very different from our early ancestors, albeit a little more complicated, and with the danger from lions much reduced. It was still a lot simpler than the complexity of life roles we know today.

Move into the 20th century and life roles started to shift much faster. Women were speaking up, demanding equal rights, insisting there was more to life than putting a hot meal on the table, and looking for options beyond running the household. Men, in turn, started to resent how their long hours at work meant less time with their families. They were looking for ways they could both be the provider and take a more active part in family life.

Part-time work was typically taken on by men nearing retirement age as a way to gradually step out of full-time work into retirement. How times have changed! According to a report released in 2016 by the Workforce Gender Equality Agency, an estimated 9 per cent of Australian men are now working in part-time employment across their working career so as to take on more family-focused roles. As national interest in gender diversity has grown, life roles and community expectations have significantly shifted for both women and men.

People are looking for and creating opportunities that will allow them to work *and* have a life. Both men and women are making different choices about family, work and relationships. Purpose and passion have become greater motivators than pay, and success is measured as much by a person's ability to balance work and family as by financial reward.

The challenge is to pursue a financially successful career while also carving out the time and energy needed to maintain a fulfilling life outside of work. In the early nineties the term *work–life balance* entered our vocabulary. Over the past ten years it has been a perennial topic of discussion in many forums. How can we achieve the ideal work–life balance? It seems as though, in acknowledging that finding the perfect balance is harder than we had initially thought, we have now moved towards a new concept: *work–life integration.*

Work–life integration recognises that life cannot always be in balance, that sometimes we have to focus on work while at other times our family takes priority, and that at times these will merge into each other, as one affects the other.

The nine-to-five, five-day work week most of us knew a couple of decades ago is now just one of a suite of work options that includes shift work, part-time, casual or contract work, and self-employment. The physical workplace has changed too, as more of us work from a home-based office or from a laptop in a car or aeroplane or even the local cafe. There is no longer one employment structure or type of workplace. Flexible work conditions and an ever-changing work environment present their own challenges for how we manage our time, our attention and ourselves. Whether written down formally or understood through unspoken agreement, whether we like it or not, we are now expected to make our work–life integration work. Technology allows us to work from anywhere and to be contactable at any time, making it hard to ever switch off.

Switching off is hard when the boundary between work and life is blurred.

Having work and life so closely connected can come at a cost. It isn't all doom and gloom though. The integration of the two sides of our lives has its benefits: it can feel good to knock off emails in the middle of the day while still in your pyjamas, or to leave work early to pick up the kids from school. On the flip side, people know they can access you whenever it suits them. You are most likely carrying your work with you in your pocket or handbag everywhere you go. Switching off is hard when the boundary between work and life is blurred.

You may establish and communicate these boundaries with clear resolve, but when you hear the ring or feel the vibration of the phone you find yourself dashing off a quick response to a work email while having dinner with your partner, or taking a work phone call while watching your child at Saturday morning sport. The justification comes easily: you tell yourself it's important and if you don't respond now it will be there waiting for you the next day, adding to your workload, so you may as well respond now. The problem is this confirms to others that you are always 'on'; they know they can contact you and you will respond, whatever nominal 'boundaries' may be in place. These messages can wait; we just need to set the expectation and boundaries ... and stick to them.

It isn't just through work that we are constantly connected. We use the internet and all its capabilities in countless ways to help us zone out and disconnect from the busy reality of our lives, and it is taking effect, as the following chapter explains.

CHAPTER 2

Constant connectivity

In her book *Inviting a Monkey to Tea: Befriending Your Mind and Discovering Lasting Contentment, Huffington Post* blogger and psychotherapist Nancy Colier suggests that society is using technology in leisure time as a way to 'numb out'. When we use technology for any other purpose than education, she says, we are simply 'distracting ourselves through the virtual world' from the real issues that are happening in our lives. We don't have to look far for evidence of this. How often do you sit and watch television at the end of the day, surfing through mind-numbing shows, while you (and your partner beside you) play with your iPad, laptop or phone, totally zoning out as a way to wind down from the day?

Losing track in the virtual world

We become so engrossed in the virtual world that we lose track of time. How often have you given yourself permission to jump online for five or ten minutes, only to find that an hour has passed? We lose ourselves in the intrigue, the information and the funny cat videos. In a society where time has become so precious, it is ironic that we will surrender so much of it to being lost in a virtual space.

Before digital technology came into our lives, at the end of a long, physically demanding day at work we would fall into bed exhausted, waking as the sun came up to start a new day. We would go to bed early, sleep deeply and wake up refreshed. Hobbies and leisure time revolved around social connection and active or creative pursuits. They were energising, based on exploration and shared with people we enjoyed being around.

Much has changed since we began to carry our personal digital devices in our pocket or on our wrist wherever we go. Increasingly we access our hobbies through our smart watches, phones, tablets and computers. Online gaming is now one of the world's most popular hobbies. The *2013 State of Online Gaming Report,* released by Spil Games, found that 700 million people worldwide (44 per cent of the world's online population) play online games.

Technology has been a wonderful vehicle for the creation of a whole new raft of hobbies. If you have ever played any of the Wii sports games or belted out a tune on online karaoke, you know how much fun technology can be. It isn't the technology itself that is causing problems; it is the behaviours we have created around our uses of technology that have made switching off hard to do.

Much technology is designed to predict our interests, allowing us to connect with like-minded people we might never otherwise have the opportunity to meet. This has led to the explosion of the social media phenomenon. The more we connect with each other, the more we want to share. Soon we find we can tap into the secret lives of our connections and through live streaming can watch them do everything from cooking to singing in the shower to busting a move on the dance floor. We have access to people's public and private lives—and people are happily giving it to us.

> The more we connect with each other, the more we want to share.

Social platform Snapchat was launched in 2011 on the promise that it was all 'about sharing moments and having fun'. For those of you who aren't familiar with it, users take real-time footage of, well, whatever they like and upload it for all to see. After just seconds the video disappears and viewers are left wanting more. According to Snapchat, users now watch in aggregate more than seven billion videos per day. At the time of writing the company is valued at $16 billion.

Snapchat's website also lists things *not* to 'snap': pornography, nudity, invasions of privacy, impersonation, threats, harassment and bullying are all off limits. Here is the one that astounds me: 'Never post or send any nude or sexual content involving people under the age of 18—even yourself'. It seems social platforms have to warn people not to capture themselves in a sexual act and then post the results to the world! Sometimes our need to be constantly connected and to amass an ever-growing list of online 'friends' has caused us to focus on relationships based on volume rather than personal and meaningful connection.

Social media and constant virtual connectedness create a context in which we live in the moment, experiencing what is happening to us right here, right now. But as we try to capture the perfect image to share with others, are we actually missing out on enjoying the moment ourselves? Are we in fact missing out on the here and now?

Again it is not the technology that is the problem but our relationship with it. The need to share every moment (or at least the good parts) isn't restricted to youths out clubbing or hanging with friends. Imagine a mother using her smartphone to capture the moment when her young son receives an award at school assembly. She immediately uploads it to the web to share it with everyone who doesn't have the good fortune to be there. Ironically, this prevents her from enjoying the moment itself. She misses the proud smile on her son's face as he seeks her out for acknowledgement, while he sees only the top of her head as she works away on her phone. In our effort to record these special moments we often actually miss them in real time. It is important to remember that being in the moment is more important than capturing it. Being constantly switched on through technology is bringing people together in the virtual world, but it is causing rifts in our real-life social relationships.

> Being in the moment is more important
> than capturing it.

Next time you visit your local restaurant on a typical Saturday night, take note of the families around you. They are probably chatting away happily about the week's events—perhaps it's a special family night out—but as soon as their order is taken and the menus removed, something interesting happens. Each family member pulls out a tablet or smartphone and starts playing on it. Mum dives into her handbag and pulls out the baby's iPad and places it on the high-chair tray. Satisfied, the parents reach for their drinks and breathe a sigh of relief... everyone is happy.

Now I don't want to fall back on that 'back in my day' line, but... back in my day when we went out for dinner (which was only on special occasions) we would retreat from the adults' boring talk by ducking under the table and making up a game to play, or we would pull out our colouring books, or the salt and pepper shakers would become an army defending the world... or we would all just sit there and enjoy the food, share stories and be thankful for being out for dinner for once. Today it seems our need to be constantly connected means we place higher importance on people and situations external to our here and now.

Don't get me wrong. The smartphone is a fantastic invention. I use mine a lot, but as a surrogate parent it is not the most effective tool. My concern is that we seem to be losing the art of connecting directly with the people who really matter to us.

The Australian Communications and Media Authority's Cybersmart Outreach Division has conducted research looking into the technology habits of young Australians. The resulting report, *Like, post, share: Young Australians' experience of social media*, published in 2013, offers an interesting insight into just how 'switched on' the next generation are. The findings showed that 11 per cent of 8- to 9-year-olds have their own mobile phone, increasing to 67 per cent of 12- to 13-year-olds. This does not include the devices they have access to at home, at school and at friends' homes. The report also found that 45 per cent of 8- to 11-year-olds use social networking sites, and this segment continues to grow despite some popular social media platforms not allowing children under 13 to create profiles. No doubt these figures will have increased further by the time this book goes to print. This reality of technological connectedness in children and young people is causing us to rethink what we know about child social development.

On technology use in children, the past president of the American Speech-Language-Hearing Association, Judith L. Page, comments: 'As adults we grew up understanding the importance of social communication and interacting with the external environment, so in a digital age where children are "digital natives" they are not having the same exposure to the important social communication skills that are developed in the early years ...'

Parents are finding it increasingly challenging to do what is best for their children's development, encouraging them to balance social interaction, learning and development of play skills while keeping up with their peers in the digital world. But it isn't just children's digital behaviour we need to watch. A survey conducted by the Pew Research Centre on the social media habits of adults found that 75 per cent of parents use social media, some spending up to three hours a day on just one networking site. So we also need to look at our own behaviours and question whether they are starting to affect the way we interact and communicate socially, as well as how they are shaping our children.

Internet addiction practitioners (yes, this is a real job description) are prescribing digital detox programs. Much as a personal trainer tailors a program for someone wanting to lose weight or to reach a fitness goal, a digital detox program might prescribe one internet-free day per week or a cap on internet usage of a couple of hours per day to help a person take better control of their internet habits, reducing the detrimental effects on their health and wellbeing. As with all things (think sugar, alcohol or high-fat foods), moderation is the key.

Wired for business

In its report *Household Use of Information Technology, Australia, 2014–15*, published in February 2016, the Australian Bureau of Statistics (ABS) found that 86 per cent of households have internet connection. For households with children under 15 years that figure rose to 97 per cent, the mean number of devices used to access the internet being seven.

Take a moment to calculate how many hours you think you spend online on any device per day and per week. Make sure you include smartphone, television (including movies), tablet, laptop and computer, in and out of work time. Complete table 1 below (and be honest!).

Table 1: hours connected

Work hours	(insert hours)	Home time	(insert hours)
Per day		Per day	
Per week		Per week	

The ABS findings showed that in a typical week the mean time spent on the internet for personal use (not work related) was 10 hours, with this number increasing to 18 hours for the 15–17 age bracket. There was no gender difference, so don't go pointing the finger!

Another interesting statistic concerns how we use the internet for work purposes at home. The ABS report found that those in management or professional positions used the internet at home more than any other sector, and that men use the internet for work more at home than women, no matter where they live.

So let's make a quick calculation. If at home we spend (conservatively) an average of 10 hours a week on the internet for private use, and we have an office job where we sit in front of a computer for eight hours a day, five days a week, that gives us a baseline of 50 hours per week in front of a computer. If we then add the time we spend checking our smartphone or tablet on the go, the hours spent constantly 'switched on' mount even further. Doctors recommend that we sleep at least seven hours per night (49 hours) per week. Sleep and internet use, then, together account for 99 hours per week. Let's say we are being good and exercising one hour each day (seven hours a week). As there are 168 hours in a week, that leaves us with 62 hours to do everything else.

> Being constantly switched on leaves us with little time to disconnect and do all the other things that re-energise us.

If you are a glass half full kind of person you will be looking at that figure and thinking, that is so much time! If you are a realist, you will be alarmed by how much you have to fit into that amount of time. However you look at it, the way we use our time is vitally important for our health and wellbeing, and being constantly switched on leaves us with little time to disconnect and do all the other things that re-energise us. No wonder our bodies are starting to feel the impact. In the following chapter we focus on the perils of being constantly switched on in the workplace, and how we can start to take responsibility for our health.

CHAPTER 3

Workplace overwhelm

As a society it seems we are trying our best to switch off more. We have apps designed to tell us when to switch off and programs to help us slow down. Workplaces are promoting healthy habits, there are government-led health initiatives, and more private companies are offering workplace-based health solutions. But the statistics indicate this is not nearly enough.

A report in 2015 by the University of Wollongong and Workplace Health Association Australia titled *Health Profile of Australian Employees* examined the health characteristics of nearly 30 000 Australian workers gleaned from workplace health assessments over the past decade. The researchers explored health factors such as smoking, levels of physical activity and alcohol consumption. Alarmingly, the research found that 65 per cent of employees reported moderate to high stress levels, with 41 per cent indicating 'at-risk' psychological distress.

A report produced in 2014 by the New South Wales (NSW) Health Department in Australia noted a significant rise in rates of overweight and obesity over the past few decades, attributing the increases to two main factors: 'excess energy intake and reduced energy expenditure', which basically translates as eating more of the wrong stuff while moving less. After a 2013 population health survey found that 51.1 per cent of adults were overweight or obese, a major government health initiative, the NSW Healthy Eating and Active Living Strategy 2013–2018, was launched with the aim of providing a framework through which key stakeholders could work together to help people make healthy choices. Noting the significant economic costs that poor health was having, the state government decided that health promotion alone was not enough. There needed to be a holistic, unified and informed approach to encouraging the adoption of healthy practices, including the promotion of health in our workplaces.

The World Health Organization (WHO) identifies occupational health as a vital aspect of an individual's overall experience of health and wellbeing. The WHO has found that workplace stress occurs where 'excessive demands and pressures…are not matched to workers' knowledge and abilities, where there is little opportunity to exercise any choice or control, and where there is little support from others'. Professor Jean-Pierre Brun, Director Chair on the Occupational Health and Safety Committee for

WHO, points to a range of risk factors that contribute to a person's health experience at work. These include:

- demands relating to tasks and roles
- degree of involvement in decision making
- employee recognition
- decision-making autonomy
- relationships
- environment and physical working conditions
- work schedules.

Expectations can serve as a powerful motivator but when unrealistic can become a source of stress and anxiety.

The expectations to integrate work and personal life and to produce more in an already pressured schedule are the main contributors to workplace overwhelm. But there are other factors that collectively can have a devastating effect on our physical, mental and social health.

Factors that contribute to workplace overwhelm include:

- the requirement to take on greater responsibility than the position specifies
- demands to do more work with fewer resources
- pressure to undertake generalist roles rather than working within skills
- the trend towards collaborative working, resulting in longer project times and unclear boundaries
- use of clients and external parties in consultative processes, calling for a greater demand for transparency and consideration

- societal demands for improved work–life balance

- juggling multiple life roles, creating time pressures at work and at home

- changing workforce expectations, such as taking work home, being contactable 24/7 and flexible work arrangements

- the fast rate of change in technology and work practices, resulting in greater uncertainty of work role and expectations

- market fluctuations and uncertainty

- the need for technological literacy

- access of patients, clients and customers to competitor value offerings and current information, meaning at times your customer may know more about your industry than you do, increasing pressure on you to remain current with all developments.

Research by the American Psychological Association and the National Opinion Research Centre at the University of Chicago explored the impact of workplace expectations on health. Their report published in 2013 found that 31 per cent of employed adults had difficulty balancing their work and family responsibilities, while 53 per cent found work left them 'overtired and overwhelmed'.

A poll conducted in 2016 by the Society for Human Resource Management (SHRM) found that burnout was one of the top reasons that people quit their job in search of a more balanced and less overwhelming position. Increasing work pressures and expectations mean people who in the past were committed and passionate about their work are becoming dissatisfied and disengaged and looking for alternatives.

The fallout of fast

Huffington Post's Arianna Huffington famously shared her experience of burnout in her book *The Sleep Revolution*. She tells of her life-changing moment when as a result of long hours and an excessive workload she literally collapsed from exhaustion, hitting her head on the corner of her desk and breaking her cheekbone. Arianna commented, 'I wish I could go back and tell myself that not only is there no trade-off between living a well-rounded life and high performance, [but] performance is actually improved when our lives include time for renewal, wisdom, wonder and giving'.

Through her willingness to share her moment of vulnerability, Arianna Huffington helped raise our awareness of the health implications for a tired and overwhelmed workforce.

Fatigue has been linked to a range of health issues such as mental health problems, asthma and heart disease, as well as performance issues such as impaired memory function, compromised decision-making skills, and reduced ability to focus and attend to tasks.

For those in high-risk jobs such as paramedics, medical and emergency personnel, and long-haul truck drivers who are required to stay awake and alert for prolonged periods in all conditions, fatigue has been identified as contributing significantly to the risk of accident and injury. In response, industry bodies across all sectors have developed fatigue management policies and best practice guidelines in an attempt to minimise the health risks and costs to organisations and the community.

Take a moment to give yourself a fatigue audit. Signs that you may be pushing yourself a little too hard and need some rest include (tick any you think apply to you):

- [ ] desire for sleep (of course)

- [ ] lack of concentration

- [ ] forgetfulness

- [ ] irritability

- [ ] poor judgement

- [ ] inappropriate risk taking

- [ ] impaired communication skills

- [ ] reduced coordination and slower reaction times

- [ ] reduced visual perception

- [ ] physical tiredness

- [ ] symptoms such as sore throat, stuffy nose or headache.

When we are busy and feeling overwhelmed we too often choose to ignore the warning signs of fatigue in our determination to complete a task or get to a destination quicker. As a result we become sick or, worse, we have a serious accident, which might have been prevented if we had allowed ourselves a little more shuteye. When we are well rested we have the ability to focus with greater clarity, make decisions with increased confidence and face the challenges of the day with more energy.

Health responsibility

Work–life integration tends to blur the lines of accountability. Who is responsible for an individual's health and wellbeing—the employee or the employer? Is the employer obligated to ensure staff are physically and mentally in shape? Or is it primarily the employee's personal responsibility to ensure they are fit to do the work? We know that what employees do outside of work hours impacts on their productivity at work. Equally, workload and workplace conditions affect how a person is able to engage in activities outside of work. Policies around health, wellbeing and fatigue management are usually adopted by larger companies with the resources to allocate to such programs. However, it is important for *all* organisations, no matter what their size, to prioritise healthy practices in the workplace—even the soloists.

There is no doubt that promoting healthy work practices benefits both the organisation and the individual. It is estimated that healthy employees are three times more productive than their less healthy co-workers and are eight times more likely to be engaged when wellness is promoted as a priority in the workplace. For most organisations workplace health programs typically start with a pre-employment medical assessment to ensure potential employees are fit for the physical requirements of the job. Unfortunately, ongoing monitoring of employee health is less common. Unless the organisation has prioritised the health of their employees, employers tend to rely on the individual to look after their own health.

Promoting healthy work practices benefits both the organisation and the individual.

Productivity is an important indicator of how well people are functioning in the workplace, but it isn't the only benefit of taking care of your staff. For the organisation a healthy workforce means:

- higher staff morale
- reduced staff turnover
- reduced absenteeism
- reduced frequency of workers' compensation claims
- reduced health care and insurance costs through sickness claims
- better performance and speed of work
- more focused and outcome-driven meetings
- a more positive corporate image that attracts healthy employees wanting to be a part of a workplace that promotes health
- improved employee engagement
- less internal workplace conflict
- committed, focused and happy workers.

For the employee the benefits of a healthy workplace are also significant, including:

- a safer work environment
- enhanced self-esteem through feeling valued within the organisation
- reduced stress and opportunities for stress management
- improved morale
- increased job satisfaction
- improved health through the adoption of healthy habits in the workplace
- improved sense of wellbeing
- positive staff relationships
- improved focus and better work output
- increased ability to make informed decisions
- greater capacity to enjoy all aspects of life, at work and at home
- better take-up of healthy lifestyle behaviours through a whole-life approach to health.

Encouraging the adoption of positive health behaviours within the workplace benefits everyone. The ripple effects of prioritising health at an individual and organisational level can be felt throughout society, from reduced healthcare costs to better family relationships and more active community engagement. When we are well, we all benefit. We have the energy and interest to play an active role in society.

> You can best gain control over your life, not by doing more, but by slowing down and taking charge.

Education, systemic change and organisational initiatives all play important roles, but ultimately health responsibility comes down to the individual level. It is imperative that individuals take control of their own health. To give your best, you need to be at your best. Simple.

You can best gain control over your life, not by doing more, but by slowing down and taking charge. So if overwhelm, overconnection and overstimulation are holding you back, then you need to learn how to slow down and switch off. In order to do so, you first need to understand the influence of your own behaviours and triggers, so let's look at this together in the next chapters.

Part II
When to switch off

At my wedding my dad stood up to deliver his father-of-the-bride speech. He looked so proud to be able to share his stories and memories of me as a child. I can still remember his handsome face, sharp suit and shiny black shoes. Dad has always had a way with words and always knows just what to say right when you need to hear it. He spoke beautifully, and thankfully made no mention of the worry I had given him throughout my childhood! 'One thing about Ange,' he shared, 'if you can't keep up with her you will get left behind.'

At the time I laughed. I knew he was right, but it was only years later that I really reflected on that comment and recognised that was how I have lived my whole life. Full throttle, full steam ahead, 100 miles an hour—I've heard them all. I have always approached life like a bull at a gate. As a child I never lived in fear, never thought, 'I wonder if…' If I wanted to do something or try something I just did. I was either all in or not in at all.

Throughout my childhood, taking charge of my life, making choices, and setting and achieving my goals at full throttle seemed to work for me. But with more life experience, more decisions made and opportunities lost, I came to realise that fast is not always best. When we live life at full tilt we get a lot done but we also tire, we get distracted, at times we even crash and burn.

When writing my first book, *The Power of Conscious Choice*, I was living life in overdrive. I was working, building a business and looking after my children while my husband worked on the other side of the country for a few months. I was trying to focus on my fitness, my career *and* my family—basically I was trying to do it all.

I had read all the books about how you can have it all, but it didn't seem to be working. Life was full, and that was the problem.

Books, magazines and online blogs are full of information on how we can slow down, take time out and find that elusive work–life balance. The idea is hardly cutting edge; it's not even new. The health, intellectual and spiritual benefits of slowing down have been recognised for thousands of years.

Buddhism, Hinduism, Islam, Taoism and Christianity, along with countless indigenous cultures, all share stories and practices around the importance of quietness and stillness, self-discovery, care for one another and the environment. These practices have been built on, interpreted and reinterpreted to apply to the modern world. In essence, though, the ancient traditions are as relevant today as they were thousands of years ago. Often we seem to fall short in our efforts to translate this knowledge into practice as we seek meaning, calmness and fulfilment in our lives, but we keep trying. With a rising interest in health retreats, corporate mindfulness programs, employer-supported mental health days, and school-based health and wellbeing programs, we are recognising the need to disconnect and prioritise our own health.

Health messages are being woven into messages delivered to children through television and film too. Movies such as Disney Pixar's *Inside Out*, Warner Bros.' *Happy Feet* and DreamWorks' *Kung Fu Panda* are all based on stories that look to educate and entertain children on important messages of mental health, confidence and finding your true self.

When we feel pulled in every direction, stepping off the treadmill to do the things we love can seem like an impossible dream. Taking the step to slow down can feel like one more thing to add to 'the list'. But slowing down is far more productive than adding another task to your to-do list.

So how do you know when you should switch off? That is the question we will explore in the following three chapters.

CHAPTER 4

Understanding your behaviours

Sensory processing and its impact on behaviour came to my attention in the early 2000s when I was exposed to the work of a group of committed therapists in Alberta, Canada, who were exploring why some children seem to find it hard to cope with everyday situations and environments. It was through working in early intervention centres for children with behavioural and developmental challenges that I was exposed to the work of Dr A. Jean Ayres, an occupational therapist and educational psychologist.

We are constantly bombarded with sensory information from our external environment and from within us. After years of research and clinical observation Dr Ayres concluded that some people find it especially hard to switch off or even modulate the signals their bodies are receiving. Her 'sensory integration theory' proposes that integrating sensory information is a neurobiological process that organises for our use the many sensations we experience through various means including touch, smell, sound, vision, taste, movement and gravity. The sensory system interprets and reconciles these signals to make sense of our environment. We then respond appropriately, but sometimes this process isn't as smooth as we would like.

Sensory overload

Sensory processing disorder (SPD) occurs when sensory signals aren't processed into appropriate responses. According to the Sensory Processing Disorder Foundation, a person with SPD 'finds it difficult to process and act upon information received through the senses, which creates challenges in performing countless everyday tasks. Motor clumsiness, behavioral problems, anxiety, depression, school failure, and other impacts may result if the disorder is not treated effectively'.

Many of the children I worked with as a paediatric occupational therapist found it difficult to cope with the influx of information generated by the sights and sounds of their physical environment. Overwhelmed by this flood of sensory information, they often struggled with typical childhood activities such as playing with their peers, learning, playing sport or being creative in any number of ways. Put simply, their ability to process sensory information was impaired. The way they showed their overwhelm was often viewed by others as bad behaviour or 'weirdness'. One child might reach meltdown in a shopping centre for no obvious reason; another might be found at a party sitting in the corner of a crowded room, eyes downcast, talking to no one. Many of us see this behaviour as rudeness, but some children's brains are simply not wired to process the mass of sensory stimuli they receive and to respond to them in a socially appropriate manner.

Sensory regulation dysfunction is the subject of some contention and of ongoing research. While it affects both children and adults, however, anyone who works with children who have these experiences cannot deny its existence or its negative impact on the way some people relate to their world. Sensory processing offers an alternative perspective on how we react to overwhelm.

Let's look at a real-life scenario. For some people, large department stores are a sensory minefield because of the overstimulation of visual, auditory and tactile experiences they provide. I admit I find such stores overwhelming, though I do not have a clinical condition. Say I'm visiting a Bunnings hardware store. It starts in the car park when we're weaving in and out of traffic as everyone competes for the spots closest to the entrance. I'm trying to watch my kids as cars frantically dart about like so many headless chickens. To add to the visual overwhelm Bunnings will often be situated next to other large department stores, which intensifies the chaotic dance of shoppers and DIYers trying to cram as much into their Saturday as they can.

Sensory processing offers an alternative perspective on how we react to overwhelm.

Then there are the smells. For some people that sausage sizzle aroma is heaven, as it typically is for me, but having barely survived the frantic car park, and facing the anxiety of negotiating the teeming aisles of floor-to-ceiling tools I have no idea how to use while watching the kids, I am quickly heading for sensory overload.

Once inside the store my kids grab the little child trolleys with the flag on top and race off, my husband is quickly distracted by the shiny tools and I am left rooted to the floor. My breathing is becoming faster and I slip into shutdown mode. There's simply too much to look at, too many choices and too much activity. I can't think clearly and I'm having difficulty articulating my words. As a way of coping I proceed to rein in the kids then follow my husband around like a puppy on a lead.

Some people, when they get to this stage of overwhelm, turn and run; others make a beeline for the cafe and retreat behind a gossip magazine. Being aware of my own sensory thresholds and triggers allows me to cope better in these situations. It allows me to apply strategies that help me switch off and either recharge or stay connected.

I know I am not alone. We all have our stress triggers and our own way of responding to them. When I hesitantly share this story with others they will usually respond with their own, not dissimilar experience—in an overcrowded pub or driving in peak-hour traffic or on a crammed bus. But it isn't just crowds or busy environments that trigger these responses. It might happen in a quiet meeting room with the ceiling fan whirring, or sitting in the lunchroom listening to a colleague chewing loudly on his sandwich, or even when emailed a 40-page report to read through. In those moments we feel our jaw clench, or the hairs stand up on the back of our neck, or a tightening in the chest. These are reactions to sensory input we do not like, and allowing them to build up over the day without being dealt with can lead to sensory shutdown.

We process sensory information in individual ways, which means we all have different sensory preferences. Some need complete silence when working; others work better with music on. Some people cherish the peace and privacy a cubicle offers; others love the energy and space of the open-plan office. For the cubicle lover, the trend towards open-plan workspaces indicates a sensory danger zone. Open-plan workspaces ensure a constant barrage of sensory information. Some people love this energetic environment, while for others it means a cacophony of overwhelm and overstimulation.

The way we process sensory information depends on many variables, such as how much sleep we have had, location, the predictability of the environment and our current stress levels. When we are more relaxed and alert we are better able to process environmental stressors and therefore to avoid the risks of overwhelm.

Let's look at how sensory build-up might affect us on a typical day.

You have had a stressful day at work. All morning you were bombarded with emails and phone calls, a meeting ran late and you were given a 48-hour deadline for a project that would normally take two weeks. You didn't have time for lunch and an accident on the road home disrupted traffic, which means you got home an hour late. As you walk in the door your young daughter screams 'Daddy's home!' and dashes out to jump on you for a cuddle, as she does every day, but today you are frustrated, exhausted. As she leaps up you snarl at her to get off you and leave you alone. The tone of your voice startles her and she turns and runs down the hall in tears. It takes you a moment to catch your breath. Still cranky, you kick off your shoes, throw your bag onto the floor and let out a big sigh. It's been a long day.

When we are more relaxed and alert we are better able to process environmental stressors and therefore to avoid the risks of overwhelm.

This scenario is not uncommon. For our unhappy dad it may have started before he even got to work. Perhaps he slept poorly the night before. Over the course of the day we build up our stress levels, and with the speed at which we are all working we are not allowing ourselves time to deal with these stresses. We move from one urgent situation to the next throughout the day, and rather than an ebb and flow of energy and emotion, we commonly experience a ratcheting up of environmental and situational stressors towards our sensory threshold. As we race between meetings, tasks and conversations we don't allow ourselves the time to adequately transition between them, to wind down and shift our energy to prepare us for what is next. Instead we just keep pushing on.

Recognise the signals

Everyone has different sensory tolerances and preferences. There is no perfect, ideal sensory profile. Our tolerances naturally change throughout the day depending on environmental stimuli. As our sensory systems become more integrated, we learn how to pay attention to important signals and tune out information that is not relevant so we can adapt our behaviours appropriately.

Looking more closely at how the brain processes sensory information can help alert us to our own triggers and thresholds and also make us more accepting of others' behaviours, maybe cutting them some slack when they need time on their own. It isn't always about you; most of the time people just need time to recalibrate and refocus.

No two people are the same. What may trigger an overwhelmed state in one person may be the perfect productive space for another, so there is no judgement here. Everyone, and I mean everyone, has at one point or another felt overconnected, overwhelmed and overstimulated. Those who recognise the triggers and step in before they take over are able to cope more effectively than others.

It is usually only when we stop and look back after a bad day that we begin to see a pattern emerge. When working with children I have encountered confusion, even sometimes conflict, between parents and teachers over the behavioural needs of a child. The teacher paints a picture of a well-behaved, obedient student who never interrupts in class. The parents' perspective reveals a different story. From the moment the child reaches the safety of the family car they kick off their shoes and start playing up or crying, and for the rest of the day the parents have to deal with the fallout from a child who has been trying to hold it together all day.

It is this prolonged restraint and final release that explain why we often get sick in the first couple of days of a holiday. You've no doubt experienced this yourself. In the lead-up to your annual leave you push yourself to get everything done. It has been a busy year. As you pack the car you are full of energy, and once on the road you are still abuzz but you can feel the calm starting to wash over you...hello holidays. You arrive and unpack the car, grab a drink, sink into a chair on the verandah and take a deep breath. The next morning you wake up exhausted and feel a tickle in the back of your throat. You push through the day but that tickle just won't go away. That night you fall asleep in front of the television and you wake up during the night in a cold sweat...Your body goes into repair mode—and your dream holiday is spent in bed.

Not allowing ourselves time to recover from, and effectively transition between, daily stressors manifests itself in both our health and our behaviours. As we'll discuss further in the following chapter, prioritising the way we transition and recover from daily stressors can have a direct impact on our health and wellbeing.

CHAPTER 5

Understanding your triggers

As we race through our lives it is easy to miss the warning signs that should alert us to impending dangers such as sickness, injury or burnout. Too often we hear of people who have been aware of a pain in their chest for weeks but have put off going to the doctor because they are just too busy—then the heart attack strikes.

Signs and symptoms

Of course these signs don't always mean we are at death's door, but they do serve to warn us that we need to slow down and take time out. Our body is the best indicator of when things are not right—we are beautifully designed like that. Signs of 'not feeling right' that can be a precursor to illness include:

- breathing difficulties
- attention deficit
- inability to concentrate
- impaired memory
- irritability
- poor judgement
- impaired communication skills
- lack of coordination and slower reaction times
- reduced visual perception
- physical pain
- tiredness
- impaired decision-making ability
- desire to be alone
- lethargy
- sore eyes
- difficulty in relaxing
- fidgeting
- abnormal bowel movements
- tightness in chest
- withdrawal from environment or physical contact

- clumsiness

- tendency to move erratically between tasks

- difficulty with task completion.

This is not an exhaustive list, and the signs and symptoms can manifest and result from many conditions. It is important you take the time to notice and listen to the messages your body is trying to send. If you are concerned about them or have been experiencing them for a while and it has been sitting at the back of your mind, contact a health professional today and get yourself back on track. When we take the time to listen to our bodies the messages can often be heard loud and clear.

Our bodies are designed to move and are capable of more than we yet fully understand. At the same time, we are also designed to rest. A healthy balance between activity and rest allows the body to perform at its best. If we persist in pushing through fatigue, upsetting this balance, we will find our body will simply demand the rest it needs, often through illness.

A healthy balance between activity and rest allows the body to perform at its best.

Beyond the physical signs that our body needs to switch off, our behaviours can also offer us useful insights into what is going on. Sometimes those behaviours can be a little scary; at other times we dismiss them as just part of life. When they become a permanent fixture in our life it is time to take stock of our health.

Behavioural indicators of when it is time to switch off may include any of the following:

- You start to feel your chest tighten when you look at social media.

- You ignore your email.

- When your phone rings you snap at it to be quiet and leave you alone.

- You don't answer your phone.

- When you hear a knock at the door you hide in the kitchen and tell everyone to be quiet.

- When asked what's for dinner as soon as you walk in the door, you yell like a banshee.

- When you think about all the things you have to do, you feel like a great weight is sitting on your chest.

- You stare at the computer screen like a deer caught in the headlights, not knowing what to do next.

- You wake up at 3 am with so many thoughts and ideas in your head that you don't fall asleep again until just before the alarm goes off.

- You are full of energy in the morning, then feel like curling up into a ball in the afternoon.

- When asked how you are you talk off topic and incessantly.

- When asked how you are you answer automatically that you're 'fine'.

- You realise your family hasn't had a meal together in weeks.

- Your children ask you when you are going to play with them again.

It is important to take the time to notice when your body or your behaviours indicate it is time to switch off, and to do something about it while you have the ability to choose.

The 3 O's

People put off going to see a healthcare professional for a number of reasons, including being too busy, not being able to access a doctor quickly enough and cost. They try to research the condition themselves. Some delay a trip to the doctor out of a fear that there might be something wrong, but the delay can come at a cost, and that cost can be your health. We all know the saying that prevention is better than cure, just as early detection and prompt action are better than inaction. If you notice physical or mental changes that concern you, it is important that you consult a suitably qualified and experienced healthcare professional without delay. Doctor Google will not cure your ailments; in fact, it will most likely add to the sense of overwhelm and overstimulation you feel already.

It is important to remember that when experiencing any of the 3 O's of overconnection, overwhelm and overstimulation you are not performing at your best, and when you are not at your best, you cannot give your best to your relationships, your work or yourself.

Doctor Google will not cure your ailments; in fact, it will most likely add to the sense of overwhelm and overstimulation you feel already.

Understanding that people generally operate in one of three key states or zones can help you to better understand your triggers and recognise the signs warning that it is time for you to switch off. The three states are:

- the Danger Zone
- the Indifferent Zone
- the Control Zone.

The Danger Zone

In the Danger Zone, as the name suggests, sickness, meltdown and shutdown threaten. When operating in this space your body and brain are in their least optimal state. This is where sensory overload and sickness will most likely occur as a result of prolonged exposure to overconnection, overwhelm and overstimulation.

In this zone you can feel irritable, tired, oversensitive, fuzzy headed. You are more emotional than you would normally be, crying or getting angry easily. Your breathing is shallow and fast, and you breathe from your chest.

Work situations, such as competing time pressures, high expectations or looming deadlines, and personal situations such as frequent arguments with your partner or dealing with prolonged behavioural issues with your children can push you into the Danger Zone.

No matter the cause, when you are in the Danger Zone you are no good to anyone. Your effectiveness is significantly diminished and your ability to make rational decisions is affected. It is crucial when in the Danger Zone that you immediately take the time to rest and recover, but notice the signs early and the negative impact can be minimised.

The Indifferent Zone

The Indifferent Zone sounds serene, but in fact you are sliding into an area that is the precursor to shutdown. Shutting down is very different from switching off. Switching off is a deliberate act: you are in control, choosing when and how to flick the switch based on your needs. When you move into physical and mental shutdown you cease to care about your health, you lack interest in your relationships and the quality of your work is compromised.

You know you are in the Indifferent Zone when:

- your head rests on the table and you refuse to do any more work

- you answer all requests with a listless 'whatever'

- you sigh deeply, with shoulders slumped (not the same as deep breathing!)

- you just want to be left alone

- you deflect responsibility

- you don't see the point of tasks

- your work output is poor

- you don't put the effort you normally would into your work or relationships

- you let your health habits slide.

When in the Indifferent Zone your care factor is zero and you do the bare minimum to get through the day. Once you hit this zone, you start to question whether what you are doing is worth the effort. People start to notice your withdrawal and lack of effort and to question your motivation and interest.

The Control Zone

The Control Zone is where it's at. This is the space where you are feeling on top of things, you have a spring in your step and life looks good. You are buzzing with energy, focused, and proactive in your work and relationships.

You know you are in this peak zone when:

- you are feeling calm and focused

- your jaw is relaxed and you are breathing regularly from your diaphragm (slow, controlled deep breathing)

- your life feels organised and in flow

- your projects are moving forward and you feel good about the progress you are making

- you feel agile and able to respond to the needs of people and tasks

- you have energy to spare at the end of the day
- you make good decisions
- you *notice* what is happening in your life and are able to adapt when needed
- you smile a lot!

The Control Zone is the aspirational space where proactive decisions can be made in all areas of your life based on what you want to achieve. In this zone you feel agile, ready to respond to the unexpected, happy and healthy.

We can find ourselves in any of these zones at any stage of our life. At times it can feel as though one minute we feel in control but in the next minute totally out of control. This is a natural part of life, but prolonged experience in the Danger or Indifferent Zone can have detrimental effects on our health and wellbeing. There are ways to move between zones, to flick the switch to prevent you from slipping into the Indifferent or Danger Zone, but first let's see where you are at right now.

Life audit

How do you think you are tracking? If you are reading this in hard copy, grab a pen and complete the table that follows. If you are reading it online or on a tablet or have borrowed the book, copy or print the table or grab a piece of paper to complete the audit.

The life audit table that follows is your chance to take stock of how you are travelling in your life right now. It is designed to give you an indication of which of the 3 O's are starting to affect you, your health and your wellbeing. Answer the questions honestly and then tally up the checkmarks in the total columns. We can then look at what the answers indicate.

Please note this is not a psychological or medical diagnostic tool and should not be used as such. Rather, it is a simple device to help you identify the things you are doing in your life that could be affecting your ability to switch off. If you do have any medical concerns, please consult your doctor or health professional.

Before we complete the table, here is a reminder of the 3 O's:

- **Overconnected:** In the context of this book this refers to an overdependence on technological connection, for example through excessive smartphone and social media use.

- **Overwhelmed:** Here we refer to a feeling of being so overloaded and weighed down by our workload that we are unable to function effectively.

- **Overstimulated:** We feel so bombarded with sensory information from our environment that we are unable to cope.

Answer the questions in table 2 by checking the 'yes' box where it applies, then tally up your total at the bottom of each column.

Reviewing your totals, how did you go? Does one column have more ticks than the others or are they fairly balanced? Do your answers align with how you are feeling in your life at this time?

Table 2: life audit table

Overconnected	YES	Overwhelmed	YES	Overstimulated	YES
Do you feel anxiety or even panic when you leave your phone at home?		Do you experience frequent tightness in the chest?		Are you breathing more heavily and faster than normal (not exercise related)?	
Do you check your phone at least every 30 minutes?		Are you becoming defensive about other people's comments?		At the end of the day (or, worse, the beginning) do you flop onto the lounge and go to sleep?	
Do you stop doing something you enjoy to answer your phone, even if it is a work call on the weekend?		Are you using language such as 'When this happens, I will be happier' or 'I'll make a change as soon as things slow down'?		Do you find it hard to concentrate in busy environments?	
Do you dread seeing your co-workers?		Is it an effort to get out of bed?		Do you find it hard to get to sleep at night?	
Do you have difficulties sleeping after being on social media before you turn in?		Do you wish you had more time for fun?		Do you long for time on your own?	
Do you find it hard to relax without using technology (e.g. watching TV, playing a computer game, being online)?		Do you have difficulty starting a new task?		Do you find it hard to concentrate when other people are around?	
Overconnected total		**Overwhelmed total**		**Overstimulated total**	

How we score in each of the 3 O's will fluctuate. A range of factors, such as our current workload, the support we are receiving and even our hormones, will play a part in how we are feeling at any particular time. Taking the time to take stock of where things may be going awry for us in a simple and honest way can unlock important answers concerning where we need to step back and where we are doing well. On an individual level, the specific factors that impact on our ability to switch off need to be explored further so changes can be made to break unproductive cycles of behaviour.

In the following chapters we will explore how you can switch off and then in part 4 how you can create a *habitat for health*, setting up your life to facilitate good health practices and allowing you to switch off when needed. Before we do, it is important to know *when* to switch on and off, and how to flick the switch.

CHAPTER 6

Flicking the switch

In a world where we are constantly 'on', being able to switch off can feel like a luxury or even an unrealistic dream. How in the world can we disconnect when we have so much to do and so little time in which to do it?

Being able to move between on and off, to transition between work mode and non-work mode, is a constant challenge for many of us. Let's be clear, though: it is not always good to switch off. A surgeon can't take time out in the middle of a delicate operation; a football player can't switch off while lining up for what might be the winning kick; a pilot can't switch off while in the middle of landing a plane. Each of them needs to be fully focused and performing at their best at such times.

There are times when we all need to be at our most focused and alert. When delivering a presentation to the executive, or listening to a client in a counselling session, or supporting a patient during their first walk after an accident, we need to be fully present and engaged. It is through being 'on' that we can direct our attention to what is important in that moment. We effectively minimise the unnecessary noise that surrounds us and adjust our behaviour to what the current situation requires.

At other times it is fine to switch off, as when reading a book, or walking along the beach. But being constantly switched off is not good either, nor is it possible in our demand-driven, fast-paced world. We have things to do and we have people who need us. If we are constantly zoned out, not exerting any effort, not involved in our communities, we lose connection. The reality is that most of us like to be active. We like to be involved, to feel we are contributing to the world in some way. The only way we can be 'on' *and* take the time needed to rest and recover is to learn how we can effectively flick the switch.

People who are at the top of their game have practised strategies that help them to be in control of flicking the switch. Surgeons require adequate intervals between operations so they turn up alert and focused. If you watch a footballer preparing to kick for goal, you will see him take position, stop still and breathe, check the range and the angle needed for the perfect delivery, pause and breathe again, and only then launch forward for the kick. And he will do this while seeming to be oblivious to the roar of 80 000 fans willing him to succeed or fail.

No matter the circumstances, the one thing they can control is how they respond to the situation they are presented with.

Professionals who understand the importance of this will hold only one person completely responsible for delivering it—themselves. Even though other factors may change: the athlete can't control the 80000 screaming fans and the surgeon can't always choose when an urgent operation is needed. No matter the circumstances, the one thing they can control is how they respond to the situation they are presented with.

Changing perspective

Professionals have a strong *locus of control*. A locus of control refers to the extent to which individuals believe they can control events that affect them. This idea was first developed in 1954 by American psychologist Julian B. Rotter, who explained that a person's locus or location could be either internal or external.

> People with a high internal locus take control of the choices they make. They own the outcome, whether or not it turns out as they intend or hope.

People who favour an internal locus of control believe that events in their lives are shaped primarily by their own actions. People with a high internal locus take control of the choices they make. They own the outcome, whether or not it turns out as they intend or hope. A person with an external locus of control believes their choices and life are controlled by factors they cannot influence or change, so when something goes wrong they blame the environment or someone, anyone, other than themselves.

Whether your default is an internal or an external locus influences the degree to which you take responsibility for your actions.

Many models of practice, such as the patient-centred model in the health industry or the customer-centred model in retail, place the needs of others at the centre of our actions. Within these models, what we do is in the service or to meet the needs of other people. What other people need is what drives our decisions and actions. Considering others is absolutely important in ensuring the work we do has meaning for our clients. A traditional patient-, client- or customer-centred model looks like this:

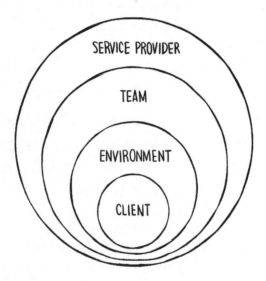

As you can see, this client-centred model places the people you work for in the centre of your actions; their needs are your focus. Decisions are made and considered based on the environment you are in—for example, you see the patient within an outpatient setting, a GP's clinic or the workplace. Working outwards, you consider the team that supports you or the people in your life. Finally, in the outer circle, there is the professional or the person delivering the service—you. You provide the direct care or service to the customer. You are the final piece of the picture. In theory this model works, but in practice it is flawed.

In a heath context, consider that a doctor spends an average of five minutes with each patient, and a typical allied health consultation lasts from 15 minutes to one hour. These appointments may take place once a week, once a fortnight or at longer intervals. The amount of attention one therapist can give a patient is limited, so this person has minimal control over the patient's choices between sessions. You could substitute any person-to-person industry here, such as retail or business, and get the same results.

Focus on you

When the customer, patient or client is at the centre of all the actions you take, you can have little or no control over their actions, and because so many factors come into play that either distract the individual or influence the decisions they make, you can have little or no impact on the outcome.

Flip this model on its head and place you, the provider or person delivering a service, at the centre of the process, and the viewpoint and priorities shift. *You* become the focus.

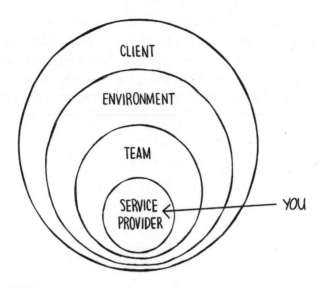

With the therapist or service provider placed at the core of the model, it becomes the responsibility of the professional to turn up and bring their best to every interaction and every situation. Why? Because it is the only thing they have complete control over. When you take full control of your own behaviour and your own health, your locus of control turns inward and you can focus on bringing your best to the situation and the people around you.

It may sound selfish to talk about focusing on you and your needs while leaving everyone else to the end, but imagine if everyone took complete responsibility for how they approached their work—their attitude, the effort they put in, the enthusiasm they showed, the priority they gave to performing at their best for the benefit of the rest of the team and clients. How different work would look with workplaces filled with responsible, committed and high-performing individuals! People who take responsibility for the choices they make. No deflecting of responsibility, no blaming, no finger pointing, just complete personal responsibility.

We can't control others, but we can certainly control ourselves.

If the locus of control is about taking ownership of the choices we make, we are placed in a position where we can choose our own actions and how we behave in any situation. We can't control others, but we can certainly control ourselves.

When we always prioritise the needs of others, putting our own needs last, we can only operate with what is left, what energy, love and attention we have left to give, leaving little for our own needs. Our energy is depleted until we have nothing left to give, and then no one benefits, least of all ourselves. When this happens it is time to flick the switch.

Our exploration of how to find calm and switch off is based on the premise of placing you at the centre of your decision making, your actions and your behaviours. The only thing you can control in your life is the actions *you* take. If overconnection, overwhelm and overstimulation are taking control, it is time to put *you* in the centre of your decision making, to use your health as the pivot point for all decisions. When you do this you become the reference point and your health becomes the foundation on which you can build. You are no good to anyone without your health and wellbeing. It is time to give your very best to everyone in your life, including yourself.

Creating useful habits

During the writing of this book I was constantly challenged by my own content. How do I flick the switch from the intense focus needed for writing to the down time I need to sustain me? Writing a book requires consistent work practices and focus, but maintaining hours of extreme focus can be exhausting. So I had to create habits that allowed me to flick the switch. Each morning I tackled a physical activity that allowed me to completely clear my head and get some energy flowing. Then I would sit for a few hours and go for it. I would have water beside me and coffee or tea and food to sustain me. I would sometimes work at home, sometimes at the office, sometimes in a cafe or sitting in the back of my car (literally in the boot) looking out over the beach for inspiration. I soon found that a few behaviours were important in helping me to flick the switch between intense focus and down time.

1. Create a work discipline

Athletes do this all the time. Each day they have a set routine they work through—no excuses. They get up early every morning and work out, come rain, hail or shine. This creates a personal expectation and level of performance they need to sustain in order to be at their best on game day. I too had to create a work discipline, even if it was just planting myself in front of my laptop, to get the work done. No excuses.

2. Listen to what your body needs

In chapter 9 we explore the importance of noticing. When developing the skills to switch on and off you need to pay attention to what your body needs. If your back is starting to feel stiff, stand up and move around; if your neck is starting to strain, stop typing and stretch; if you are feeling tired, rest. By doing this you give your body time to recover and re-energise to take you forward.

3. Change environments

One of the benefits of today's more flexible work practices is that many of us have the option of working from anywhere or at least moving between different environments as needed. If you need inspiration, move somewhere else. This might be to a different desk or to a completely different location where you know you can either focus better or switch off better. I would often walk to a local cafe in the morning, set up my laptop at my usual table and write for a few hours. I produced more work there than in any other place. Perhaps it was the mix of the people around me and the peaceful yet energised environment, and the delicious coffee helped! I would go there when I needed inspiration and focus. Then the half-hour walk back to the office would allow me time to switch off and prepare to switch back on as soon as I reached the office.

4. Set time parameters

Facing tight deadlines and at times unrealistic expectations, we constantly feel pressured by time. It feels like there's never enough time to get anything done. Adopting time goals

(continued)

Creating useful habits (*cont'd*)

or boundaries helps us to flick the switch between on and off. Traditional to-do lists offer no parameters for how long things will take. We know that on any task we will fill the time we are given, but it is amazing what we can achieve when given a deadline. So set a realistic time frame to complete a project, and don't give yourself an out. Focus for the time you have set yourself, and as soon as that time is up switch off and move on to the next project. This is an effective way of managing time, managing your focus and getting the job done.

According to Dr Jenny Brockis, an expert on brain health and high performance thinking and author of *Future Brain*, being able to effectively shift attention is about recognising the signs that the brain is starting to fatigue and then giving it the rest it needs. 'When we stay focused on a task too long our brain becomes tired, particularly if we haven't given it adequate rest. There are warning signs that the brain is moving into energy conservation mode: for example, our mind wanders off task; we have difficulty articulating words; or the speed at which we process information slows.' Dr Brockis explains that when this brain fatigue occurs we need to bring our conscious awareness to what is happening and shift our mind space, much like pressing pause, to disassociate from what has been happening to this point and move to a different state of mind. To flick the switch from intense or prolonged focus to a more relaxed state of mind and to move on with clarity, we must slow down our thinking.

Part III
Regaining control

My aim in writing this book was not simply to reinforce everything we already know. We all know we should eat healthily, move more, sleep more and do work we love. These messages are delivered to us through newspapers, television, the internet and the conversations we share. I can recall sitting in a cafe writing on my laptop (thank you cafes with free wi-fi, by the way, you rock!) when the table next to me was taken by a group of mums with their small children, all (mums and children) dressed head to toe in activewear. They parked their prams, extracted their children and sat them at the smaller table next to theirs. They proceeded to hand each child a tablet (the computer kind) and offered them the choice of a babycino, smoothie or juice.

As a side note, I can remember in my pre-children life being appalled by the idea of a babycino—who would give their children coffee, even a small one?—before I learned that a babycino is actually not a mini latte but simply frothed milk with a sprinkling of cocoa on top, or if you're lucky a dash of chocolate topping.

The mums duly placed their order, and once the three two-year-olds were happily (and silently) playing Candy Crush on their own iPads, one of the mums opened the conversation: 'I can't believe how tired I am!'

So started a half-hour, three-way conversation on the pitfalls of motherhood, coping with small children at home, trying to stay fit, finding time to hang out with friends and grappling with the challenges of starting a business. Yes, I was eavesdropping, because at the time I was writing about the very things they were talking about. Between their sips of coffee and iPad sounds, what I was really hearing was the common challenge of how to integrate all the things we know we need to do into our busy daily lives. They knew they should be encouraging their children to play together, but at least the tablets kept them occupied and quiet. I wasn't about to pass judgement on them—as a mum I have used the iPad as a babysitter at strategic times—but if we know we should be encouraging our children towards active play and real social interaction with other children, why don't we?

It's one thing to know what to do, but it's quite another to know *how* to do it. Part III is about how we can take what we know about slowing down and apply it in our life—day in, day out. When life is so busy, how do we make this work? How can we switch off and still get done what's needed? Here we'll look at some practical ideas and strategies on the most effective ways to flick that switch. So together let's turn you off!

CHAPTER 7

We can choose

Have you thought about what it will be like to face death? It is one of life's great unanswered questions: what happens when we die? People talk about seeing a light, being welcomed at the 'pearly gates', falling into darkness. Those rare individuals who have been at death's door and returned report different versions of the experience. When we arrive at that point and look back on our lives, what achievements will we be most proud of? What will we wish we had done differently?

In her book *The Top Five Regrets of the Dying*, palliative care nurse Bronnie Ware reflects on the insights she gained through her patients' stories about what they looked back on with regret as they neared death. Bronnie shares the five most common regrets of the dying:

1. I wish I'd had the courage to live a life true to myself, not the life others expected of me.

2. I wish I hadn't worked so hard.

3. I wish I'd had the courage to express my feelings.

4. I wish I had stayed in touch with my friends.

5. I wish I had let myself be happier.

These regrets are beautifully simple yet offer us a poignant reminder that when we look back on our life at the end, it is generally not with a wish for more, but a wish for less. Less comparison with others, less work, less fear, less isolation.

When we feel overwhelmed, overconnected and overstimulated it is easy to lose touch with what really matters to us. We feel we need to do more with our lives. When we are stuck in a web of comparison, life is lived outwardly and we forget what we really want to be doing in our own lives. No one wants to live with regrets and we all want our lives to be happy and healthy, surrounded by people we love and who love us, so why do we keep pursuing more? On our deathbed we won't look back with pride on a life spent in pursuit of more, but rather on a life well lived, no matter how long or short. So instead of worrying about impending death let's look at how to live a full life without regrets.

 Take a moment right now to reflect on Bronnie Ware's list. If you knew you would die in a week's time, would you admit to any of these regrets? If so, what could you do over the next week to make it right and reduce your sense of regret? Look back on your life and ask yourself, what have I been doing that has created this regret? If you have lost touch with your friends, why? Has being constantly busy resulted in you not having the time to pick up the phone and connect with a friend, or are you so focused on your family that friends no longer seem like a priority?

Write it down, it helps a lot.

Taking control

The 'worked too hard' regret is one of the main reasons I wrote this book. Most people work too hard and are often exhausted. If this is you and you want to stop it, read this book right through to the end!

Looking at all of the regrets, one theme that stands out is that they are all things we can choose to change. They are not beyond our control—in fact they are all well within our control. So how can we make the changes needed?

In my book *The Power of Conscious Choice*, I look at how we can take control of our life through bringing awareness to the choices we make. One thing we all want in our lives is the feeling that we are in control of it, not that life happens external to us and we are simply pawns being moved around at the whim of others. When we are overwhelmed, overconnected and overstimulated, knowing how to stop feeling that way can actually add to our worries, bringing us down on ourselves for not having the answers...and so the cycle continues. It can feel awful knowing that things are not working for us and change needs to happen, while not knowing how to make the change.

When we are beset by the 3 O's it isn't as simple as just deciding to change. This is the starting point, but there are a few more steps to take, and it all comes down to how you make decisions.

Have you ever reached a decision you thought was logical but your gut told you otherwise? It just didn't 'feel right'. This is because the decisions we make in our lives derive from a mix of logic and intuition. Logic is based on information; intuition is based on feeling.

Choices define the actions we take in our lives. Each choice we make builds on the last and moves us towards the next choice. Our decisions are part of a flow of choice making that is always an exercise in coping with an unknowable future. No amount of deliberation, analysis and time can guarantee that we have identified the perfect option or the best next step. This unknowable future can generate fear when it comes to making a decision, which can stop us from making any decision at all. This is when it can seem as though life simply 'happens' to us, or nothing at all happens, and we move through life passively.

Making better choices

A proactive life means making a choice then acting on it based on the information we have—and it feels right. So how can we make better choices?

When faced with choice, we typically consider our options, weighing up the pros and cons and gathering enough data to make us feel confident that the choice we make is the right one. For some this process is long and drawn out, while for others a good night's sleep is enough.

A proactive life means making a choice then acting on it based on the information we have—and it feels right.

Decision making commonly follows a pattern:

1. We examine the facts related to the choice to be made.

2. We create space by taking a break from logical thinking to allow our intuition to take over.

3. We bring the information together with our values.

4. We make the decision.

Decision making involves six key stages in a continuous cycle: *think, feel, decide, do, reflect* and *choose again.*

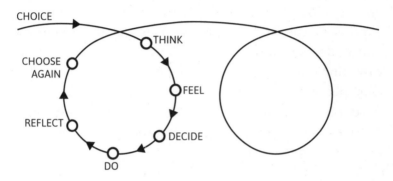

Let's work through this list using a job-changing scenario. If it helps, apply a particular situation you yourself are facing right now.

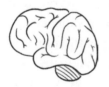

Stage 1: Think

It is at this first stage of the continuum of choice where most people feel the best choices are made. This is where the logic behind our decision making comes into play. At the think stage we weigh up options, analyse data, check baselines, consult experts and gather as much information as we can.

The think stage can become complicated and time-consuming, but it is important. Before we can make a good decision we need all the facts. If you are looking at changing your job, you need to understand the competitive environment, your financial situation, what jobs are available in your industry and a potential exit strategy from your current position. You have to collect all the facts and understand the numbers, otherwise you could end up losing out on employment conditions, or you might find you lack the skills needed. With an endless array of data, blogs to read, research to wade through and experts to consult, this process can feel overwhelming. Our brains become so crowded with information that we can't think straight. It is at this point that you will often hear people say, 'I just need to step away from it,' or 'I need a break from it'. What this means is the information overload is starting to creep in and they need to move on to the next step.

Stage 2: Feel

At the feel stage we reflect on how the options we have been presented with align with our personal, cultural and organisational values. How do we feel about the choice we are considering? Intuition means 'going with your gut' rather than using logic. It can't be explained rationally. It is sometimes described in spiritual terms such as 'the universe leading you' or 'being shown the way'. It just feels right or, as my mum would say, you 'feel it in your waters'.

Intuition is not commonly spoken about in business, particularly in corporate environments, as it is generally viewed as a 'soft' skill that has no place in strategic decision making. But therein lies a problem. Logical decisions leave out the emotional aspect, yet we all know that consumers base their decisions predominantly on emotion. You might choose to buy shoes that are quite uncomfortable and way too expensive but look amazing, or to lash out on that really cool looking surfboard, even though you don't know how to surf! We do this sort of thing all the time.

Going back to the job change scenario, if you act purely on emotion you can end up making a decision that is too risky and could have a negative impact on your career or personal situation. Intuition-led decisions that ignore logic can cause problems. If we go into a decision based purely on emotion without thinking it through, we can end up ignoring important facts. Logic and intuition must go hand in hand if good decisions are to be made. And this needs time.

> Logic and intuition must go hand in hand if good decisions are to be made.

But allowing time for decision making is becoming more challenging as we struggle with the faster pace of work and life, and as a result we are making ill-informed or lazy decisions. Sometimes the best choice is right in front of us, and if we allow ourselves time the answer becomes glaringly obvious. We may reflect later, 'It was there all along—why didn't I see it?'

Stage 3: Decide

It is when we integrate what we know with what we feel that we make our best decisions. Relying only on information gathering or waiting for it to 'feel' right can result in a missed opportunity. Recognise the point at which a decision must be made one way or the other, make that decision and then go for it. You'll know pretty quickly if it was the best decision for you or the situation. Back to our scenario, there will come a point when you need to decide whether or not you are going to leave your job. Continuing indecision may result in a lost opportunity; on the other hand, staying just where you are might be the better option.

> It is when we integrate what we know with what we feel that we make our best decisions.

When faced with choice, we can spend too much time thinking and not enough time doing. We become paralysed by the details of our plans, opportunities and options. This is often called *paralysis by analysis*.

Sometimes all you need to do to break out of a state of indecision is take one small step, but at other times it will need a big step, even a leap, to really shake things up. This might mean leaving a comfortable, well-paid job to re-spark your passion for the work, or ending a relationship that is not serving you well, or even packing up and moving house. Whether it's a small step or a big leap, take the time and create the space to make an informed decision that best suits your needs.

 ## Stage 4: Do

With so many distractions in life, creating change can be hard. Deciding you want to change jobs is a start, but following through on the decision is another thing entirely. It is the actions you take each and every day that make the difference. Getting up early and doing a morning workout, preparing meals for the week and going to bed earlier—these things take discipline. Creating good habits will bring your decisions to life.

Stage 5: Reflect

By the reflection stage you have weighed up your options and made your decision and are out there making things happen. You are getting a sense of whether the choice you made was the best one. You now have the advantage of hindsight to show you whether or not your decision served the purpose as you had hoped.

Time for reflection is important. In our right here, right now world we are quick to move on to the next thing. Organisations that allocate time for reflection on the impact and outcome of decisions make good decisions again and again. They identify what they did right and what they did wrong, and use the experience to shape how they approach similar situations in the future.

Reflection needs time, but not necessarily a lot of it. It can be as simple as a Friday afternoon review of the week or as detailed as a consultative review process. The point is that insightful reflection can only occur if you step back from the process to look at it objectively, to notice and observe.

If you want change, you need to
do things differently.

In a fast-moving world, reflection is the most overlooked part of the continuum of choice. Rather than learning from past decisions, people just keep moving along. Be warned: without reflection you will keep making the same types of decisions, whether they turn out to be good or bad. If you are looking to create behavioural change, then heed the words of Albert Einstein: 'The definition of insanity, is doing the same thing and expecting a different result'. If you want change, you need to do things differently.

Stage 6: Choose again

By this point on the continuum, the process of choice may have felt like it was too fast or a very long, drawn-out process. In the previous five steps you have:

1. gathered information

2. listened to your intuition

3. made the decision to do nothing or commit to change

4. dug deep, got your hands dirty and brought the decision made to life

5. taken time out to reflect on the outcome of your choice so you can heed the lessons learned.

Every choice we make opens the way for another, and another. So this last stage both completes the cycle and starts a new one. Based on our experiences, and the lessons learned, we get to make another choice and continue to control the direction we take.

In an interview with Julia Gillard, the first female prime minister of Australia, Melbourne *Age* journalist Samantha Lane asked what were the biggest lessons she took from her time in the top job. Surprisingly, the response was not a standard 'I wish I could do more for my people'. Ms Gillard said she would like to have 'retreated more often into a cone of silence'. She went on to share how in an overly connected world urgent tasks on our to-do list constantly vie for our attention, making it 'harder than ever to carve out the thinking time, the quiet time, the unplugged time, to work out what is important, rather than just attending to the urgent'. With the gift of hindsight, I wonder what different decisions she might have made throughout her leadership if she had allowed herself more time for reflection.

With greater insight into how to make good choices in life based on understanding the cyclical nature of the decision-making process, we can now start to make better decisions on how we switch off when we need to.

Introducing the phases of switching off

It can often feel like the only way to switch off is to step away completely and opt out of life until we are rested and re-energised, ready to step back into the fast lane again. Most women will admit that spending time at a health retreat holds a position on their bucket list. And why not?

You travel to an exotic location, up in the mountains perhaps. You wear activewear all day. All your nutritionally balanced meals are prepared according to the cycle of the moon. You wake to the sound of birds chirruping in perfect harmony and are greeted by a buffed masseur ready to tend to your every need over the course of the day. In the yoga tent you are welcomed by another tanned, muscular god named Sven who will help guide you through a long session perfectly matched to purge both body and mind of tension and stress. No pressure, no deadlines, no one else to think about, only you... (Note: factual details have been changed to protect the author. You will not find Sven at every health retreat.) Ahhh, the serenity!

If only we could just stop and step off the crazy treadmill of our lives and take up permanent residence in a health retreat. Wouldn't life be perfect? Well yes, it would be fantastic, but what about your family, your children, the work you love, your warm comfortable bed? Escaping 'normal' life is a great way to switch off and reconnect, but the reality is most people do not have the opportunity or means to attend a retreat whenever they feel stressed.

Working there won't solve the problem either. Naturopath Laurel Barron has spent more than seven years living and working in health resorts in exotic locations, the types of places most of us could only dream of visiting. Fascinated, I asked her what it was like to live like that. Does she get to have massages whenever she wants, eat three perfectly balanced meals each day, use the state-of-the-art gymnasiums these places boast of? Naive as I may have been, her response shocked me a little. Yes, the settings are beautiful and serene, and working with people who understand the importance of health and wellbeing is special, but the work can be exhausting. I tried to keep the mockery out of my voice. 'Oh poor you, it must be so hard…' But Laurel's explanation made sense.

'Working in a retreat, the days are often long. You're working with people who have come to escape busyness, so it is your job to make sure they pretty much don't have to do anything, which means you have to do *everything*! Working in day spas in particular can be tiring. We want to ensure the best experience for visitors so we give them all our energy along with their treatments so they leave feeling revitalised and refreshed. Which means at the end of the day we ourselves will often feel tired and drained. But fortunately we have the tools to deal with that!'

This conversation with Laurel set me thinking. If escaping to live in the mountains is not the answer for most of us, how can we integrate the skills of switching off into our daily lives so we can do what we need when we need it?

At times in our lives most of us will find the overwhelm becomes so great that we wish we could reach for a big red stop switch sitting right in front of us, like the safety cord on a treadmill, ready to pull when we can't keep up. When we get to this feeling we often need to do just that—stop and get off. Unfortunately switching off is not as simple as pressing the big red button, to be instantly revitalised and refocused. The great news is that switching off doesn't mean doing more… it means doing less!

Together we are now going to work through the phases of how to switch off—how to move from feeling overconnected, overwhelmed and overstimulated to feeling in control.

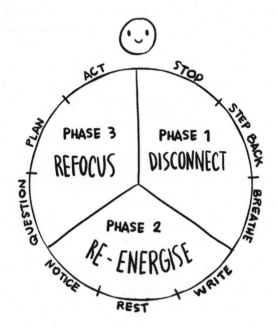

CHAPTER 8

Phase 1: Disconnect

The hardest part of switching off is taking the first step of simply stopping. You have already stopped to take the time to read this, so high five to you. Take a moment to take a big, deep breath and slowly breathe out. Come on, don't resist it. Breathe in, breathe out. How nice does it feel to just stop? We will explore 'the power of breath' in a moment, but for now let's embrace how great it feels just to stop.

Stop

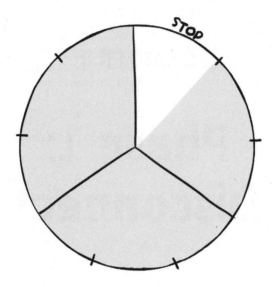

If stopping feels so great, why don't we do it more often? The simple answer is we do, we stop a lot. We have many moments when our body is 'still'—when we're watching television, sitting at our desk at work, lying in bed. Our bodies are still more often than we might think. So what are we complaining about? Well, there's stopping and there's *really* stopping. Most often when we are sitting idly in an effort to switch off, our mind continues to race. We try to slow down while still engaged in stimulating activities. We watch television while on our tablet, we go for a time-out coffee during which we respond to email, we push our kids on the swing while talking on the phone. Despite our best attempts to slow down, in reality we often don't wind down at all but only build up further overstimulation. When we do this we are not fully in the moment; we are merely distracting ourselves from the here and now. While trying to switch off we embrace activities that ensure we are still switched on.

So how do we really stop? First we have to recognise the need to. We use time pressures as the reason we can't switch off. How often do we say we don't have time to go for a walk or to call a friend, yet when we get the phone call from the school to say our child is sick or our doctor says we need to slow down or we will have a heart attack or our car breaks down on the way to work, we find that after all we *are* able to make immediate changes to our schedule. When something more important and urgent presents itself, we shift things around.

> While trying to switch off we embrace activities that ensure we are still switched on.

If you are longing to stop for a while, block out the time and do it. Rework your schedule, say no to a couple of things or take yourself off to a location where no one can reach you, and give yourself a break — even if it's only for a few minutes. If the stress of your work day is compounding and you can feel the tension increasing, shut down your email for ten minutes and just sit and think, flick through a notepad and draw, take a walk, hide in the stairwell if you need to—just give yourself a chance to stop and disconnect. The more such small opportunities you give yourself, the more you can reduce the compounding effects of daily stressors.

Step back

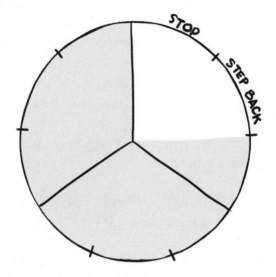

First, good on you for exploring the idea of stopping. It is liberating even to think it's possible. Next time you think to yourself, I need to stop … do it. Once you have stopped, it is time to take a step back from the immediate demands that are competing for your energy.

We often grapple with challenges in our life by digging deeper for solutions, gathering more information in order to find ways to resolve the issues. Counterintuitively, we respond to being overwhelmed and overstimulated by doing more. It just doesn't make sense. Doing more is not the answer. We need to take a big step back to gain perspective.

Spend some time in a local art gallery and rather than looking at the art, watch how other people view it. They stand in the middle of the room and scan the walls in search of a painting that takes their fancy. They take a step to the left, a step to the right, crouch down, tilt their head or simply stand and stare. When they are ready they slowly move closer to the chosen work to take in the detail — the brushwork, texture, craft. When they have looked at it from close up for a while, they step back again to appreciate the beauty of the whole painting. If they looked only at the detail they would miss the full beauty of the composition.

Translated into our own lives, when we are caught up in the daily grind of our to-do list and never lift up our heads long enough to gain a broader view, we miss the full picture. We fail to appreciate the effort we have put in, the skills we have mastered, what we have achieved. We lose perspective when caught up in the detail. Finding the time and space to step back can feel out of our reach, so we are drawn into overwhelm and negative thinking. All we can think of is how hard life is, how we are too busy, too stressed, too frantic. How much easier it would be if we just slowed down. Only by taking a step back and gaining perspective can we create the space to choose how we fill our time and apply our energy.

How to take a step back

- Say no more.

- Remove yourself from situations you don't want to be involved in.

- Say yes to a friend who offers help.

- Go out for dinner with your partner to just talk.

- Get comfortable with delaying requests for help by answering, 'I'd like to but not right now'.

- Be open to asking for help or delegating.

- Try something outside your comfort zone that you wish you could do more of.

- Turn off phone notifications. Constant distraction fragments our attention.

- Sign out of social media so you are not tempted to just 'do a quick check'.

- Set technology parameters. Google Chrome extensions such as Block Site and StayFocusd, and programs like Freedom and SelfControl, allow you to control technology and how you use it.

Breathe

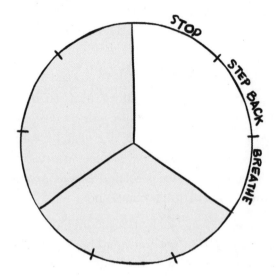

The health implications of breathing techniques have been increasingly recognised in recent times. The importance of breathing has been documented in books and articles addressing conditions such as asthma, depression, insomnia, chronic pain and stress. Books such as *The Power of Your Breath* by Anders Olsson and *The Healing Power of the Breath,* by Richard P. Brown and Patricia L. Gerbarg, have argued for the health benefits of our 'breath' and how this applies to modern living, offering a drug-free solution to common stress and mood problems.

When we are physically or emotionally stressed we hold tension in our bodies: we clench our jaw, raise our shoulders, hold our breath. Both traditional and modern medicine have demonstrated the existence of a deep mind–

body connection. Our body registers what is happening in our mind and our state of mind is influenced by what is happening in our body. That is why we are more likely to experience physical ailments or the flare-up of an old injury when we are worried or upset.

Stress is costing us. A 2014 global meta-study by the European Agency for Safety and Health at Work found that stress-related health conditions are costing governments from $730 million per year here in Australia to €617 billion across Europe. These astonishing figures show that combatting stress-related health problems is an overwhelming international challenge.

With stress having such a fundamental impact, could breathing techniques offer one small but significant piece of the puzzle of how to reduce our daily experience of stress?

Simply put, breathing is a way to stop, slow down and reconnect to self.

Harnessing calm, deep, paced breathing is not a new-age, hippy practice. It has been practised as a daily ritual for centuries across many cultures. It is a central aspect of Buddhist meditation, yoga and the Chinese practice of Qigong. Christian monks use breathing as a way to bring awareness to the body to calm the mind, heal the body and focus on establishing the body–mind–soul connection. Simply put, breathing is a way to stop, slow down and reconnect to self.

It has so many other benefits too:

- It keeps us alive!

- It regulates blood pressure, circulation and heart rate.

- It strengthens our immune system.

- It improves quality of sleep (and you won't get kicked out of bed for snoring!).

- It helps your body to effectively burn energy from food.

- It improves sex drive.

- It helps us to cultivate a sense of calm and relaxation.

- It helps us to manage our physical response to stressful situations.

Joseph Pilates, who founded the practice of pilates in the early 1900s, placed great emphasis on breathing techniques and mind–body awareness because he observed how people who practised his methods experienced improved health. Today, pilates is being used around the world by millions of practitioners in small studios, dance centres, gymnasiums and therapy clinics and at home. With ever higher expectations and demands for speed and efficiency in the way we work and live our lives, the importance of focusing on our breathing to help us to slow down has become even more critical.

Pilates, yoga and meditation all demand a conscious awareness of our breathing patterns. Indeed, a focus on the breath is often the starting point for teachers of these disciplines. The approach to breathing varies with each practice: one modality might focus on nasal breathing; another on long, deep breathing through the mouth; another might engage sound. Whatever the method, each discipline focuses on 'the power of the breath' and bringing our conscious awareness to it.

Because breathing is largely unconscious, we tend to take its power for granted, forgetting its importance, but by becoming more aware of our breathing we can learn to improve our body's function and performance.

The frequency or rate of our breathing changes depending on the pressure we put on our cardiovascular system, such as when we undertake high-intensity physical activity. It can also be increased by psychological factors such as stress or when we are surprised or nervous. Fast, shallow breathing is typically associated with moments of high stress on both the body and the mind.

When we breathe more slowly and deeply in a controlled way, with every deep breath we take we experience an increase in carbon dioxide, which prompts the dilation of the cerebral blood vessels and increases the oxygen supply to our brain. This promotes calm and a feeling of increased awareness and alertness. Slower breathing is good for us, particularly in those times when we are feeling overwhelmed and overstimulated.

Tess Graham is an Australian physiotherapist and founder of BreatheAbility International, an organisation focused on improving our wellness through breathing techniques. She teaches, 'To sleep well and be well, you must breathe well. This is just a simple law of nature'.

So if breath is the very thing that gives us life; the importance of breathing properly has been known for centuries; and these techniques have been shown to have significant physical, mental and even spiritual benefits, why are we not giving them the attention they deserve?

Physiotherapist and pilates instructor Jenna Kennedy believes it is because of our 'no pain, no gain' attitude to health that we feel we need to push ourselves to the limit to gain maximum benefit from any fitness session. 'In my practice I have witnessed people walking into their first class expecting a grunt-and-groan style session,' Jenna shares. 'Instead, they are welcomed with information about their breathing and an introduction to creating an awareness about how their body is feeling. This important awareness of breath and tension in the body is crucial in creating a strong foundation on which we can build flexibility and strength to overcome injury or chronic pain.'

We can start to train ourselves to exercise greater control of our breathing, not only in a fitness class or on a yoga mat, but also in daily life when we experience stress or tension.

Slow, controlled breathing increases our physical energy by balancing the chemical exchange of oxygen and carbon dioxide. Focusing on breathing also helps to minimise external distractions and turn our attention inward. As we try to slow down and step back, it is a great time to turn our focus inward to the thing that drives us and sustains our energy — our breathing.

If you need help with these techniques, consult a practitioner who understands the importance of breathing well and can provide you with the tools and strategies you need. Integrating them into your own life is a great way to prepare for the next phase, which is to re-energise yourself.

To channel the best advice on how to move from fast, high, shallow breathing to calmer, more controlled and deeper breathing I have enlisted the expertise of physiotherapist and pilates instructor Jenna Kennedy:

Simple breathing routine

Watching a clock, place your hand on your chest so you can feel the chest expand and relax. Over one minute count how many times you complete one breath cycle (breathing in and out is one cycle). Make a note of how many breath cycles you completed in that one minute.

To put functional and effective breathing in perspective, a good rate of breathing is between 10 and 14 breaths per minute. How did you do?

You can control the speed and quality of your breath. If you feel as though you are breathing from your chest only, try the following activity to shift to a deeper, more controlled breathing pattern. You will feel instantly calmer.

Deep breathing routine

Sit comfortably on a stool with shoulders and chest back and relaxed. Place your hands on either side of your ribcage, take a big breath through your nose and be aware of what you are feeling through your ribcage. Feel your ribcage expand as the breath moves through your nose. Notice the expansion and the depth of your breathing.

Slowly breathe out through pursed lips. This will help you to control your breathing. You will feel your ribcage move inwards.

Allow your hands to move with it, applying a little pressure. This will give you a long, slow out-breath. Aim to breathe in over four seconds and then out over four seconds.

Repeat this sequence four times.

Return to your normal breathing pattern for four cycles. Then, placing your hands back on your ribcage, try another controlled cycle. Repeat the whole process another four times.

At the end of this you should be feeling as though your breathing is both deeper and more controlled. You will also feel a sense of calm and focus. This routine can be done anywhere at any time, and the number of cycles can be changed to suit the time you have available.

CHAPTER 9

Phase 2: Re-energise

Now we have taken the time to stop, step back and breathe, we can start to rebuild our energy reserves. How we do this is not by getting straight back into hectic activity. Maintaining a slower pace through the re-energise phase will ensure the benefits are more profound and longer lasting. If we look at the way a house is built, much initial time and effort are allocated to laying the foundations. It is an overused analogy but a relevant one here: build the foundations well and you will have a solid base on which to build. The same applies to re-energising yourself. Take the time to switch off and you will have a base from which to start to move forward with habits that serve you well.

Write

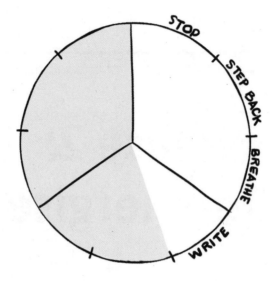

Thoughts, feelings and insights have always been shared through the power of storytelling. Passed down orally from generation to generation, stories have shown us how the world works and pointed to what is yet to come. Stories, passed on orally, through images and the written word, continue to be a powerful form of communication. Bloggers share with the online community their thoughts and ideas on everything from potting seedlings to fixing a printer to making sense of how the universe works. We are swamped with so much information that we often feel overwhelmed. And the online community continues to expand every day. I won't even attempt to calculate how many online blogs are active, as by the time I finish writing this page hundreds more web pages, social media accounts and blogs will have been created.

It is understandable why so many people feel they need to share their innermost thoughts, fears and dreams, ideas and observations with a global audience. The internet gives us all a platform on which to write and express ourselves. In earlier times no such platform existed. We had ochre and rock or ink and a feather quill or pen and paper to communicate with a relatively limited audience. Now we have a platform that allows us to share these intimate thoughts with the world.

Being able to share and communicate our thoughts and feelings is important in allowing us to work through the issues currently troubling us or to help us make sense of our current situation. Sharing our thoughts allows us metaphorically to step back from the issues that concern us. One way we do this is through the practice of journaling.

For some, journaling may conjure up images of teenagers writing awkward love poems to their high-school sweetheart and recording other secrets never to be shared. But in the digital world its use has become more common than you might expect. Now scientific research is being conducted to find out exactly how writing impacts on our thoughts and feelings, and the effect it has on our physical and psychological wellbeing.

From a range of research into areas such as emotional intelligence, goal setting and self-confidence, it appears that the benefits of journaling are as immediate as putting pen to paper. Making journaling a habit has been linked to improvements in creative thinking, immune function, memory and communication skills, for example.

The practice of mindfulness, now a mainstream idea, the explosion of adult colouring-in books, and journaling point to three popular approaches to helping us switch off. People journal in many different ways. For some it is a daily ritual to clear the mind of the day's activities and thoughts. Others use it as a tool to help work through challenging situations or to deal with emotions experienced in relation to a particular incident or event.

Call me old school, but I love to grab a pen or colourful pencils and a notepad and get lost in my often busy brain, scheming up my next adventure or big idea, or perhaps just reflecting on how I feel right now.

I am very conscious of the benefits of writing down my thoughts on paper when I am feeling emotionally overwhelmed, as well as the many ideas I have floating around in my head. I had always thought this was a practice I developed later in life, when life became busier and its demands greater. Then one day, while wading through a box of treasures from my childhood passed on to me by my parents, I came across a brightly coloured A5 notepad with Winnie the Pooh on the cover and a padlock on the side. The find flooded me with emotion and happy memories of the secret world of my childhood. On the first page I had written the date...I was 14 years old when I started that book, and to my delight it was full of positive quotes from the great motivators, like Dale Carnegie, Napoleon Hill and Winnie the Pooh himself. Deeper into the book I found hand-drawn set moves from training, complete with every type of short-corner combination, from my most loved sport, field hockey, along with words of advice from my mentors and coaches. It was like reopening the doors of my 14-year-old mind. Even as a young teenager, it seems, I had known the benefits of writing down my thoughts and ideas to help me think clearly and switch off.

You may well have your own version of journaling or recording your thoughts. If you don't, let me share with you a simple technique to help you use the power of writing to clear your head: it's called *brain dumping*.

The human brain is an amazing, complex system, and it can be a challenge to make sense of what is happening inside our head when it feels full or fragmented. With overstimulation the brain becomes 'fogged', and unless you metaphorically step back from it, it is hard to gain perspective.

The simple act of brain dumping is your secret tool to prevent brain overload.

With too much information to take in, too many decisions to make and too much to remember, the brain becomes overloaded and trying to think clearly can be exhausting. The simple act of brain dumping is your secret tool to prevent brain overload. For this exercise you will need a notepad and pen, or your tablet with a writing app.

Brain dumping

Step 1: Get writing

Using your writing tool of choice, start to write down everything that is in your head. Don't worry about making relationships or connections between the ideas. Unload whatever is going on there. Resist organising the information, just write it down. The purpose of a brain dump is simply to get your thoughts out and onto the page. If you only have a couple of thoughts knocking around in your head, it means either there is not much happening in your life or some big priorities are taking up most of your brain space right now. If you have enough to fill a whole book, then go for it—the pages are sure to make interesting reading.

Step 2: Breathe

Yes, here is an opportunity to practise your breathing again! Having dumped all of those thoughts filling your head on paper, you should already start to feel lighter. Taking a breather will help you to reset your body and move into action mode. So ... breathe. How does that feel?

Getting all of that stuff out of your head is a big feat. Now what do you do with it?

Step 3: Connect the dots

Dump done. Breathing done. Now it's time to start making connections and to draw out relationships between your thoughts. The beauty is that now you don't have to try to navigate through the mess inside your head. You can take a step back from it all (remember, stepping back helps us gain perspective), see it more clearly, and start to slice and dice.

How you take this step is up to you, but here are a few suggestions: grab colour pens, felt-tip pens or crayons, and use the same colour to circle all the concepts that are related. For example, thoughts may be connected by time or an area of your life, such as work or family. You will notice that your jumble of words begins to acquire some order. Once these relationships have been made, choose a form that suits you and organise your thoughts into categories accordingly: draw a mind map or a table or write a list. As you impose form and categories, so your jumble of words become coherent ideas that you can action as needed.

(continued)

Brain dumping (*cont'd*)

Step 4: Lock it in

This is a book about how to switch off; it isn't a book about how to do nothing. Switching off is important because it gives us the energy and focus to switch on when we need to. To make a brain dump worthwhile you need to take what you found in the previous step and prioritise what needs to be done. Not everything will be a priority. Most ideas can wait, so place them on a wish list and you can get to them later. Look at what is most urgent in your brain dump and complete that first by going straight to your calendar and blocking out the time to do it. Keeping those big priorities in your head can add to the overwhelm and leave you feeling like you don't have the time or space to do anything.

Step 5: Breathe again

Well done, that's it! You have cleared your brain, giving it the space it needs to work its magic. The more often you do brain dumps, the quicker and easier you will find it. An initial 20-minute exercise can eventually turn into a two-minute, end-of-the-day, space-clearing activity.

Journaling and brain dumps create important cognitive space, giving us more space in which to think clearly and be creative. It is as though we have given ourselves a blank canvas on which we can start to create whatever we choose.

Rest

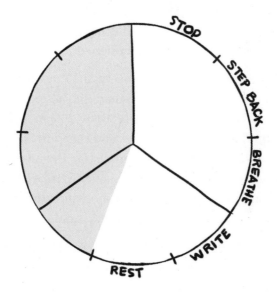

Sleep and rest are often viewed as luxuries in our fast-paced world. With so much to do and so little time, sleep and rest are seen as obstacles to getting stuff done. If we stay up late we can cram more into our schedule; we can stay connected through social media long into the night. If we get up early and start our work day early we can get more work done...before we get to work.

Sleep psychologist Professor Dorothy Bruck, at the Sleep Health Foundation (SHF), is concerned that people are increasingly using the bedroom, the room dedicated to sleep and intimacy, for activities 'such as emailing, searching the web and watching movies, all activities that are not conducive to sleep'. Being constantly connected in the bedroom is having negative effects on our quality of sleep, and encroaching on the time and energy we need for the other fun things bedrooms are designed for!

An SHF study found that more than 18 per cent of adults report regularly sleeping fewer than six hours a night and that sleep disorders affect more than 20 per cent of the population. The amount of rest and sleep an adult needs varies according to the individual, but the average adult needs seven to nine hours a night. After a full night of good-quality sleep you will feel happier, healthier and more alert.

Give yourself a quick sleep review. How many hours a night have you slept over the past week? Fill in and total the middle column in this table.

Table 3: sleep review

	ACTUAL SLEEP	RECOMMENDED
Monday		6–9 hours
Tuesday		6–9 hours
Wednesday		6–9 hours
Thursday		6–9 hours
Friday		6–9 hours
Saturday		6–9 hours
Sunday		6–9 hours
TOTAL:		**42–63 hours**

Note: Seek medical advice if you are concerned about your sleep quality.

Are you getting the recommended hours of sleep at night? If not, think of this as a little wake-up call. Side-effects of being sleep-deprived include:

- lapses in attention
- reduced ability to stay focused
- reduced motivation
- reduced ability to make informed decisions
- compromised problem-solving ability
- confusion, irritability and memory lapses
- impaired communication skills
- poor assessment of risk
- faulty information processing and judgement
- slower reaction time
- indifference and loss of empathy
- reduced ability to fight illness and infection
- added direct healthcare costs through the management and treatment of sleep disorders
- workplace health and safety costs associated with fatigue-related incidences.

Fatigue contributes to side-effects beyond just feelings of sluggishness and an inability to come up with a good idea. A range of costs have been identified that have a significant impact on us both personally and as a community. Harvard researchers estimate that sleep deprivation costs the United States $63.2 billion in lost productivity every year. The SHF reports that fatigue and poor sleep cost Australia $3.1 billion in lost productivity each year. These staggering figures could be much reduced if we committed to balancing activity with rest.

We all know the importance of sleep and taking a break when we are starting to feel overtired or ill. The problem is, rest is typically what we do when it is too late—we rest when we are already overtired and/or sick.

Fatigued workers perform at sub-par levels compared with their well-rested colleagues. In military training exercises, recruits are deliberately deprived of sleep and rest and are put in stressful situations where they are required to solve complex problems, undertake physical challenges and decipher important messages. The point of such challenges is to mimic the real-life scenarios found in time of war, when personnel could expect to be sleep-deprived yet still need to make split-second, life-or-death decisions. These sleep-deprivation exercises demonstrate how basic tasks can become complicated, or even impossible, when we are denied adequate sleep or rest.

Google has long been famous for the range of staff benefits it offers, including providing sleep pods to which tired workers can retreat for a quick nap before returning to the job, rested and re-energised. Google management have used research knowledge of the benefits of sleep to help foster an alert, creative and productive workforce.

Wouldn't it be nice if your employer encouraged you to sleep on the job! The reality is few of us have the luxury of working under such a regime, but fatigue management does not have to be as radical as this. Responsibility for ensuring we are well rested, and recognising that fatigue management is an important part of productivity, safety, health and wellbeing, rests with employers, managers and employees.

The challenge for employees, particularly those who are paid overtime rates for additional hours worked, is to see beyond the financial incentive to the risks of working when overtired.

Policies around management of work fatigue vary across sectors, states and territories, with no single set of guidelines that employers must follow. This poses a challenge for responsible employers, who must try to understand the recommendations of current research on managing fatigue in the workplace on top of all of the other safety, health and operational factors that come into play in business.

Safe Work Australia recommends that employers undertake a range of actions to help minimise fatigue in the workplace, including:

- ensuring sufficient cover is provided for workers who are on annual or sick leave
- limiting overtime to four hours for eight-hour shifts
- designing rosters and work practices to reduce fatigue
- having a policy on second jobs—ensuring workers understand the obligation to get sufficient sleep and be fit for duty
- creating fatigue policies to mandate the importance of employee fatigue management
- promoting two hourly breaks of at least five to ten minutes' duration per shift
- encouraging healthy eating practices at work by providing access to healthy food options.

Fatigue management is also the responsibility of the individual. Each of us must ensure we have adequate, good-quality sleep. This is easier said than done for busy people, but the impact of fatigue on work performance and our lives is too significant to ignore. If quality sleep is a challenge for you, here are some ideas to help you sleep more soundly.

- Create a relaxing evening routine that prepares you for sleep time.

- Create a bedroom environment that relaxes you: quiet, dark, comfortable, and no television or tablet before sleep.

- Avoid caffeine, alcohol and other stimulants before bed.

- Try to go to bed and get up at the same time each day. Yes, this means no long Sunday morning sleep-in!

- Plan your social activities to ensure you get sufficient sleep between work shifts.

- Buy an alarm clock, and leave your phone in another room.

- Do a brain dump before you turn in at night. Write down what is on your mind; once the information is out of your head, you won't be tossing and turning throughout the night thinking about it.

Getting the rest you need is also important, and this doesn't just mean sleep. You don't need to allocate hours to this; it can be as simple as a 15-minute disconnect by having lunch outside, sitting reading a book or flipping through a magazine. When you are feeling under pressure and need a quick injection of energy, before you reach for an energy drink or sugar-laden snack understand that sometimes your body is telling you simply to switch off for a few minutes.

One of the most effective ways to switch off is to create good sleep habits.

To rest means to 'cease work or movement in order to relax, sleep, or recover strength'. So when you walk in the door at the end of a busy day, if you need to kick off your shoes and flop on the bed for ten minutes, do it. If you need to grab a cup of tea and sit on the verandah and stare off into the distance for a while, do it. Take opportunities to rest when you can, and when these opportunities are integrated into your day you will find you can take shorter rest breaks and still gain the benefits. Most workplaces now have regulations about rest breaks so make sure you take these breaks, and take responsibility for your own energy needs by taking micro-breaks when needed.

Here are some ideas on how you can switch off through taking a break.

Ways to take rest breaks during your day

- Every 20 minutes of sitting, get up and take a short walk or move away from your workstation. Walk to the water cooler, for instance.

- Every 20 minutes look away from your computer and look into the distance to give your eyes a break.

- Do frequent stretches at your workstation.

- Go outside to eat your lunch.

- When you finish a long call, take four slow, steady breaths.

- Intersperse computer work with phone calls, written work and meetings. Your body and your mind will love the variety.

- When taking public transport, read something unrelated to work to rest the brain.

- At the end of the day, take off your work clothes and change into fresh ones. This helps with the transition from work and will make you feel immediately rested.

The busier our lives become, the more the effects of fatigue are being felt in our workplaces, our hospitals and our homes. The message is clear: for safer, more productive workplaces, and happier, healthier people, rest and fatigue management is a priority. Resting is the single most effective way for you to switch off and gain the energy boost you need.

Notice

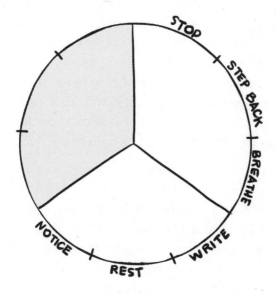

For thousands of years indigenous people have embraced the importance of slowing down to observe what is happening in their surroundings. They knew through observation that when the stingray are fat certain plants are in bloom, or when the dragonflies are about the dry is coming. This knowledge came about not through Googling or sourcing other people's opinions in social media chatrooms. They did not have specially compiled information sources at their fingertips to answer their every question. They learned about the seasons, about nature and about the relationships between them simply through taking the time to notice. They sat, watched and listened. Through this direct experience they learned about and appreciated their environment, the natural world, their culture and themselves.

English broadcaster and naturalist Steve Backshall, a modern-day pioneer in furthering our knowledge of nature and our environment, once tracked an endangered Bengal tiger for five days in the hope of merely catching a glimpse of it. Why? Because it is through watching and observing that he has identified animal behaviours and traits that have not previously been observed or understood.

Child psychology is another area where an emphasis on observation has allowed us to enhance our knowledge—in this case, of how children develop their play, and their social and physical skills. Psychologists observe groups of children at play to determine how they behave, how they interact and how they problem solve. Based on observation and the simple act of noticing, studies in child development have significantly enhanced what we know about the ways and speed at which children develop.

The challenge for most of us is to find the time to sit and notice. With the mantra 'time is money' driving our businesses, idle time that generates no direct income is considered wasteful and non-productive. This couldn't be further from the truth. Taking the time to notice provides us with valuable insights into the way the world works, the way we work and what is happening in our lives. Through active noticing we gain insights into our business, our customers' experience, our families, and the people and world around us. Watching and listening, we can switch off from the chatter inside our heads and the overstimulation in our lives.

To notice without learning or applying what we learn is to be a passive observer simply watching the world go by.

For those of you who are still not convinced, I'm not talking about sitting around all day doing nothing. To notice without learning or applying what we learn is to be a passive observer simply watching the world go by. Noticing time is productive time, as the nuggets of insight you gain in these moments add to your understanding of the world. The things you learn will spur you on to make changes in your life, helping you to understand others better and create space where you can find opportunity, new ideas or clarity.

The ancient art of meditation

Meditation helps practitioners to notice what is occurring within themselves. For a long time I resisted meditation, convinced I would find it impossible to turn off my hyperactive thought processes. Of course I knew it was a practice some thousands of years old, which had to give it some credibility. Finally I vowed to give it a go. What I discovered was a discipline that allowed me to tap into the world around me and within me. It seemed all of those millions of people who practised it were onto something!

In essence, meditation is the act of resting the mind and attaining a state of consciousness that is quite different from the normal waking state. The practice takes many forms, and there is really no right or wrong way to achieve the state.

Dr Emma Seppälä, Science Director of Stanford University's Center for Compassion and Altruism Research and Education and author of *The Happiness Track*, has researched the area extensively. Among the effects of meditation on our body and our mind, her scientific analysis identified:

- increased positive emotions

- increased life satisfaction

- improved immune function

- reduced experience of pain

- reduced inflammation in the body

- increased memory recall

- increased ability to self-regulate and control emotions

- improved quality of meaningful social connectedness

- increased ability to empathise and show compassion

- improved resilience

- reduced stress, anxiety and depression.

All of these benefits are derived from the practice of being still and present that lies at the core of meditation.

Shivani Gupta, founder of Passionate People Institute and author of *Passion @ Work* and *Tough Love for Leaders*, helped to dispel any lingering doubts by showing me the profound impact the daily practice of meditation can have on our ability to make decisions, our productivity and our sensitivity to the signals that warn us to slow down.

Shivani believes there are three common reasons why people do not adopt meditation practice: the first is a lack of understanding of the profound benefits of meditation; the second is the perception that you need lots of time and a dedicated space in which to meditate; the third is not knowing what to do once you decide to integrate meditation into your life. 'Meditation needs to be simple,' Shivani explains, 'easy to do and practised regularly so it becomes a part of your day. The more you practise meditation the easier it becomes to clear your mind of the chatter and the "stuff" that so commonly fills our minds.'

Simple meditation techniques

If you have always meant to give meditation a go, or are even just curious, Shivani offers three simple meditation techniques we can all use, no matter how busy we are. In only five or ten minutes each day you can calm your mind and re-centre yourself when you are feeling caught up in the overwhelm of the day.

Technique #1

When your head is full and you are feeling overwhelmed or overstimulated, the simpler the meditation practice the better. Sit somewhere quiet or at least somewhere you can disconnect a little (so don't do it in front of the television).

Close your eyes and breathe in slowly through your nose to the count of four, then slowly breathe out through your nose to the count of four, and repeat as needed.

This is an effective technique when you are feeling overwhelmed or overstimulated as it gives you a fast result and you can do it anywhere, even when sitting in your office or while having lunch. Super simple and super effective.

Technique #2

This technique works when you have a little more space in your mind and are not as overwhelmed but still want to calm yourself. It requires more visualisation than the first technique, so you need to be a little more open to using your imagination.

Sitting, imagine you are a tree (stick with me here!). Place your feet flat on the ground and visualise roots coming out of the bottom on your feet, spreading long and wide into the ground.

Picture feeling the stability and feeling grounded, and use the image of the roots as a strong way to reconnect to feeling supported. Sit in this position, holding this image in your mind, for five minutes. As thoughts come into your mind let them pass through and stay focused on holding the tree image. The visualisation will help you feel less frantic and more grounded and stable.

Technique #3

This third technique requires a little more focus than the other two, and some people might find it a little 'out there'. Do this when you are feeling more focused and less frantic, using the technique as a way to top up your reserves of energy. We all radiate energy, and through this practice we make sure the energy we give out is positive. At the end of 5–15 minutes of doing this you should feel happier, calmer and filled with renewed energy.

Sitting comfortably, picture the energy centres (chakras) within your body. There are seven of them, positioned at the base of the spine, the lower abdomen, the upper abdomen, just above your heart, the throat, your forehead just between your eyes, and the top of your head. Focus your attention on a light of positive energy passing through each of the chakras and bathing them with radiant light. Watch the ball of light make its way to the top of your head and out into the universe, taking any negative energy with it.

For some people this might feel a little spacey, talking about chakras and balls of light. If you prefer to look at it another way, just sit and picture a ball of positive energy working its way up through your body, filling you with good energy and cleaning out the negative energy.

As noted, one of the main reasons people do not meditate is a perceived lack of time. They feel they simply do not have the opportunity to sit and think about nothing. But think about this: on average we spend 1.72 hours a day checking social media status updates, which are all about how other people are living their lives. Surely then we have a few minutes a day to sit and turn our attention inward so we can refocus our own energy.

Finding stillness

Meditation is not the only way we can slow down and gain the clarity of mind needed to notice, but regular meditation practice creates a foundation for us to build upon. It is like giving our mind a daily spring clean.

Here are a few things you can do that will help you to start noticing how fortunate you are in your life.

- Put your phone in your bag or your pocket so you are not walking around with your head down. Look up and around you.

- When you are at the park with your children, sit on the bench and watch them. They are fascinating to observe, and before you know it you will have the energy and enthusiasm to jump on the slide with them.

- When you are taking a lunch break, go outside, sit down and watch the people around you as they hurry about. You'll see people wearing headphones, eyes front, powering along like they were in a race. You'll start to notice just how fast we are all living and think about how much we miss out on through all this rushing.

- In a meeting take time to sit back in your chair and notice the dynamics in the room. Who is talking the most, and who is not saying anything? What is really going on behind what is being said and unsaid? We can learn so much in meetings by drawing back and simply noticing. When the time is right, step into the conversation. After watching and listening to the conversation your ideas and responses will be considered and timely, rather than rushed and pressured.

- At home at the end of the day, grab a cup of tea and relax out on the verandah. Don't read or use a device, just sit and notice. Watch the birds, listen to the noises and look up, down and around. You may see things you have never noticed before.

- When your children read to you, watch their faces. Notice how perfect they are. Admire how their brains are working and be happy knowing you helped to create these masterpieces.

Noticing is taking the time to connect with our surroundings so we can gain a new perspective on the world in which we live. By noticing more we gain valuable insights into the people in our lives and, more importantly, how we fit into the world.

CHAPTER 10

Phase 3: Refocus

Another high-five coming your way! By now you should feel like you have the tools and strategies to switch off when you need to. You should know how to take a step back when required and how to create the space to think and rest.

In phase 3 of switching off we flick the switch. We can't always be in a zoned-out, disconnected, chilled-out rest zone. Now it's time to draw on the perspective and energy we have gained through taking time out and to plug it in where it's needed. But before we get too excited let's take the opportunity to shift our focus to how we are going to do things from this point forward. We were brave enough to stop, we were willing to open ourselves to noticing what is happening within and around us, and we learned how to surrender ourselves to being well rested. Now is the time for us to ask, 'Knowing what we know, what are we going to do about it?'

To be effective we need to know how to flick the switch.

Generally, this sort of reflection is dismissed as a waste of time. We hear the saying, 'The past is past, the future is in the future. What matters is the here and now'. And this is right...in a way. But if we don't take the time to look back at our experiences and learn from them, we will often keep on repeating patterns of behaviour that do not serve us well. When we focus solely on moving forward we don't take the time to identify these patterns and make the changes needed. This final phase is about refocusing and bringing into our lives the energy to spur us to do what we need to do. To be effective we need to know how to flick the switch. When we can do this, we start to regain control. But first we must be honest with ourselves about what we want.

Question

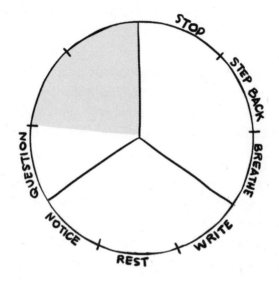

Remember when we looked at the continuum of choice back in chapter 7? In stage 5 we explored the importance of reflecting on decisions made. This stage is important in breaking negative cycles of decision making and facilitating opportunities for great decision making.

Moving into this phase you need to ask yourself key reflective questions about how you have been doing things in your life, so you can make the best possible choices about when and how to switch off from this point forward. You don't want to wait until you are sick or exhausted to switch off; you want to be in control of when you take time out and how you use your energy and focus. If you really want to embrace the lifestyle that comes with being able to flick the switch when you need to, first take the time to look at why this lifestyle matters to you and how the benefits of living a life of being in control will allow you to do the things you love with the people you enjoy being around.

Five key questions will be important in helping you to take the next step towards creating positive change in your health and your life. Think of them as starting points for further exploration. How you answer these questions will be absolutely key in taking you forward, so grab a pen...

1. What have you learned about yourself during the process of switching off?

2. What did you find was the most challenging aspect of switching off?

3. What is the one thing you can implement today that will help you to switch off when you need to?

4. What difference will the ability to control when you switch off make in your life?

5. How prepared are you to make the changes needed to prevent you from feeling overconnected, overwhelmed and overstimulated?

If you don't yet feel ready to answer these questions and are just flicking through the book for valuable information, it would be a great idea to flag this page; put a sticky note on it or insert a bookmark so you can come back to it when you are ready. Don't wait too long though, because your answers to these five key questions are what will move you into feeling calm and in control.

As already noted, the process of switching off is determined by personal variables. When answering these five questions take notice of how you are feeling, particularly when responding to number 4, 'What difference will the ability to control when you switch off make in your life?' The feeling you get will tell you a lot about how important it is to make these changes in your life now.

Plan

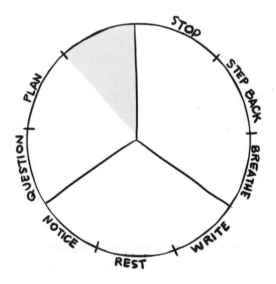

Armed with the strategies and skills to switch off when needed, it is time to refocus on how you are going to integrate this knowledge into your daily life. Switching off from work, life and people is a process. Incorporating the skills in your life takes practice, and it becomes easier when you have a plan.

> Without a plan or map we are feeling our way blindly, which means we rely on luck, past experience and other people to show us the way.

Throughout this book we have talked about the importance of the simple daily habits we create and the profound impact they can have on our sense of being in control of our lives. Without a plan or map we are feeling our way blindly, which means we rely on luck, past experience and other people to show us the way. Taking the time to create a map of how we want our lives to look, the direction we want to head in and what targets we want to meet — that is, what we want to do in life — will significantly increase our ability to achieve these goals. It doesn't mean we'll always achieve them, but with a plan we can start to make choices based on where we would like to go.

Plans can be as specific or as loose as you like. Whatever you choose, draw from what you have learned through the phases of switching off, taking into account your financial, personal, health, family and relationship, and work plans. Your plan will mean more than setting aspirational goals as it draws on the lessons you have learned through switching off and creating the space to think, create and reflect.

In the final chapters of this book we will work through a map of how to create a *habitat for health* in your life.

I'll also introduce some tools to help you build the energy and drive you need to fulfil your goals and live the life you choose.

Act

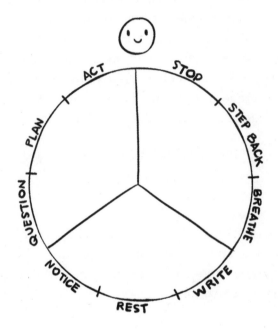

This needs the shortest explanation of all phases of switching off, yet like the first phase, Stop, it is hard to do. It is the habits you implement each and every day that will make the difference when it comes to effectively creating the energy and space needed to switch off and then flick the switch. The hardest part is having the willpower to turn off the television and go to bed earlier, or to get up a little earlier to practise meditation or to create the space to practise breathing more effectively.

As Charles Duhigg explains in his book *The Power of Habit*, 90 per cent of our actions are habitual. Create daily habits that serve you well and motivate you. Rather than trying to overhaul your whole life or change ten things at once, start with one action and focus on that until it becomes a part of your day. Once the practice becomes a habit, add another. Overcommitment, trying to make too many changes at once, sets us up to fail. It is all too hard. We become overwhelmed and revert to our old, familiar habits...and so the cycle continues. Just choose one thing that will make the biggest difference for you and go from there. We don't want to make change any harder than it has to be!

Create daily habits that serve you well and motivate you.

It's time to discard old habits that have not been serving you well, that have led to your feeling overconnected, overwhelmed and overstimulated, and to start to make choices and develop habits that give you the ability to flick the switch when you need to.

Part IV
Designing your habitat for health

We have looked at why switching off is important and strategies for accomplishing it. The hard part is putting what you have learned into practice in your own life. I hope while reading this book you have tried out some of the tips and strategies. If so, how did you go? Were the strategies as simple to realise as promised? Did you find some of the challenges you came up against easy enough to work around?

The chapters that follow are designed to show you how to integrate these new skills into your life. The key is to create an environment around you that allows you to flick the switch in the simplest way possible.

Most people follow daily practices to help them do their work, run their household or stay healthy. As a society we are obsessed with the habits of the rich and famous, perhaps imagining ourselves one day becoming super wealthy and successful, like Virgin's Richard Branson or Zappos' Tony Hsieh or Facebook's Sheryl Sandberg. At the click of a button we can read about the habits that helped make them successful. In just over half a second Google will deliver more than 400 000 search results for 'Richard Branson's success habits'!

So the scoop on the habits of successful people is easy to find, and it turns out that they're not that complicated. They are things like getting up early, sorting out their priorities and writing their to-do list before starting work, keeping up to date by reading the newspaper, keeping fit by taking the dog for a walk, going to the gym or practising meditation—all before most of us have even woken up. Author Steven Pressfield writes in his book *Turning Pro*, 'The difference between an amateur and a professional is in their habits'. The habits will vary with each individual, but what they have in common is these people's dedication to maintaining them. No matter how tired, cranky or unmotivated they might feel, they *never* allow their success habits to slide, and neither should we. The easiest way to ensure this is to set ourselves up for success.

CHAPTER 11

Setting up for success

Through my work as a mentor I have met many very intelligent, capable and resourceful people who for one reason or another were so overconnected, overwhelmed and overstimulated that it was getting in the way of their health. I have always found common threads in my clients' stories: they all know what to do; they just need someone to remind them how to do it. Leanne was one of them.

A single woman in her late twenties, Leanne came to me looking for help to break through some of the barriers that were keeping her from switching off. She was sick of feeling tired and flat, lacking 'get up and go'. She described to me what would typically happen to her each time she found the motivation to start a new 'health kick', as she called it.

Over the weekend she would decide that on Monday morning (it was always a Monday morning) she would focus on her health again. Her plan was to get up at six every morning to exercise — no program, she'd just do what she felt like doing. She always intended to eat better, give up takeaway food and prepare healthy snacks rather than buying her lunches. She was a bit of a night owl and knew she had to turn in earlier, so she resolved to be in bed by nine o'clock. She imagined reading a book for a while before falling into a deep sleep, then waking up refreshed and eager for her six o'clock exercise session.

It rarely worked out that way, she confessed. She shared with me her most recent attempt to reduce her work stress and start to focus on her health.

She felt ready, so despite not having much food in the house she decided to start first thing Monday. Come Monday morning the alarm went off and she heard the sound of light raindrops on the roof. It was a little cold so she decided to hit snooze…a couple of times. Eventually she rolled out of bed to hunt for some clean clothes to go for a walk in, preferably something that 'didn't have rips or holes in it'. She got changed and after ten more minutes of searching for her phone holder (she likes to listen to music while exercising), she finally got out the door with only 15 minutes to spare before she had to start getting ready for work. She was determined not to fail the first morning though, so 15 minutes was going to have to do.

Back from her walk, Leanne found she was famished. She checked the fridge for the ingredients for her breakfast omelette (she'd once heard they were good for her), except she hadn't bought groceries; she usually shopped on the way home from work. There was nothing much in the fridge so she grabbed a 'breakfast on the go' bar, thinking that would be 'healthy enough'. She didn't have time to make lunch, so she ended up buying it.

At the end of the day, she had to stay back at work to finish a project. By then she was so hungry she decided it was too late to get groceries and cook, so she grabbed a takeaway meal and took it home to eat in front of the television, where she eventually fell asleep. She had no idea what time she fell asleep but she woke at 3 am to find the television still on. She wandered off to bed, forgot to set the alarm and woke again at 7.30, with no time for a morning workout or breakfast.

Leanne admitted this was not a one-off, that a similar cycle had happened more than once before. She had concluded that focusing on her health was just too hard and decided she was 'not meant to be healthy'. What she couldn't see was that right from the beginning she had set herself up to fail. She had no plan and no systems in place to allow her to achieve success. She had the best of intentions, but her planning and execution were terrible—actually she had no plan to execute!

Leanne's story is a common one. At one time or another you may have had a similar experience. You resolve to make a positive change in your life, but you just don't get it off the ground. You have every intention to make it work, but it just doesn't.

Most of us know the important ingredients of a well-rounded health and wellbeing program. It isn't a lack of knowledge that is the problem, as a Google search will present you with a vast range of ready-made programs to support you on your journey to health. Access to information is not the issue. Motivation is not normally the issue either, as you are probably super keen to get started. The real challenge in starting a new health regime or embracing a lifestyle makeover is *preparation*.

Motivation was certainly not Leanne's problem, and she knew what she needed to do to make healthy changes. What let her down was her failure to take the necessary steps to set herself up to succeed. She didn't do the legwork and create an environment that would support an easy transition. As we look at how to create a habitat for health in the following chapters, keep Leanne in mind. Think about what she could have done to make her health journey a success.

> We all need to create a habitat for health, an environment that facilitates positive lifestyle choices.

It is important to understand why creating the right environment is so important in ensuring your health success. We all need to create a habitat for health, an environment that facilitates positive lifestyle choices. With a habitat for health you can be in control of your health and wellbeing even when you are busy, tired or unmotivated. *Habitat*, as defined by Dictionary.com, is 'the natural environment of an organism; a place that is natural for the life and growth of an organism'. A fish's natural habitat is water, a lion's is Africa's grassy plains and open woodlands. Our habitat is our home and the places where we work and live. If we are determined to take control of our health and wellbeing, we need to establish an environment that supports our life and growth.

We need to create our own personal habitat for health complete with all of the tools required to support it. How do we do that? So glad you asked. Get your pen ready because this part of the book is where we move from learning into action. Together let's create your very own habitat for health so you can switch off and on whenever you choose!

CHAPTER 12

Your picture and your people

It will often happen that when you walk into a room you will consciously or subconsciously take a deep breath. Maybe you love the space and feel at peace in it (and your breath is calm and happy) or maybe you find the space confronting or overwhelming (and your breath is drawn in from shock or unease). This initial breath is a cue to determining whether or not it is an environment you like to be in. Compare, for example, the feeling you get when you walk in the door leading to your workplace (if you don't totally love where you work) with how you feel when you step through the front door at home after a long, stressful day. The feelings are very different—one stressful, one calming.

Create your picture

What we are aiming for here is to create an environment where you feel inspired, energetic and prepared for whatever comes your way. Whether you work from home or an office, being in an environment that inspires you will help you be more focused and creative. Let's start creating that place where you feel inspired, energetic and at peace.

1. Draw your habitat

With a pencil in hand, draw a picture or write a description (whichever you prefer) detailing what your home would look like if it had everything you needed to help support your health. Would you like a refrigerator full of fresh fruit and vegetables, or would you like all your meals pre-prepared for the week ahead? Would you like a gym area set up in the garage or a running track nearby? Organisers and boxes with labels on them so you know exactly where to go to find your things? Trendy activewear in your wardrobe that makes you feel great when you put it on? Whatever it is, draw it or write it down. You can also do this activity for your office or workplace—wherever you want to create a habitat for health. Here is a little prompter for you to get you started.

2. Create your map

Within the picture you drew of your ideal habitat for health (or your written description), circle the items you do not have already, the things you will need to buy, set up or start doing. If you want a gym set up at home, do you need to buy a weight bench, a treadmill, a yoga mat? If you want to prepare your meals in advance, do you need to buy more containers or a recipe book full of healthy pre-prepared meal ideas? Breaking down each area or action into easy-to-achieve steps will make them seem less daunting. You may even find that your ideal habitat for health requires just a few simple changes.

3. Prioritise the list

Now rank the items you circled from highest priority (1) to lowest. The highest priority should be ascribed to the thing that would have the biggest positive impact on achieving your health goals. Then work your way through the list.

4. Set your top three

Take the top three items/actions from activity 3 and write them in priority order. For each, think about if you were to take that action or make that change, what difference or impact would it have on your life and the achievement of your health goals.

Now that you know how to make the list, why not try making one yourself. Using table 4, fill in the gaps to make your own top three (the first row gives an example).

Table 4: setting your priorities

Priority	Action/Item	What difference would it make?
	Buy a gym set.	I can exercise when the kids are in bed, and I don't have to travel to the gym.

5. Make it happen

Over the next two weeks take the highest priority in row 1 and make it happen, make the change, buy the item or set up the system. Then try it out. It is important not to do everything on the list at once, as it will most likely be too much to manage. Take the top priority and try it out for at least two weeks. If you need longer then stick with it; if you are finding it simple to adhere to then add the next action, and so on. Before you know it, your habitat for health is coming to life.

Creating a 'picture' of your habitat for health is an important way of both clearing your head and keeping you focused. It is a vital activity when looking to implement change, as it lays the foundations that are crucial to creating positive health habits. You create the picture on which to build. Just as you need a plan when building a house, you need a visual map of what your ideal health environment looks like. If you are unprepared or have unrealistic expectations, it is hard to develop and stick to a viable plan. By drawing a detailed, realistic picture of your ideal environment from the start you are setting yourself up for success.

Establish your health team

The people who come in and out of our lives play different roles. Friends give us support and friendship; colleagues offer professional guidance, skill development and camaraderie; family provide love, acceptance and a sense of belonging.

Surrounding themselves with positive influences is the secret to many prominent business leaders' success. Successful people commonly attribute their success to the dedication of an enthusiastic support team or to working alongside people 'smarter' than them. Think of Apple's 'two Steves'. Steve Jobs was the visionary, the front man and the driver behind Apple's success. Steve Wozniak was the maestro behind the technology that created and powered the company. They were yin and yang, but together they changed the face of digital technology and communication.

Whether through a formal mentoring relationship or occasionally meeting with a colleague for a coffee to share ideas, the value of having people who can support your personal and professional development is often underestimated.

In our habitat for health, the people we surround ourselves with are vital to our success. Truly successful people never do it alone. In an interview with *Forbes* magazine, Chairperson and Chief Executive Officer of PepsiCo Indra Nooyi spoke of how she found her way to the top seat at PepsiCo through surrounding herself with a 'tribe of people'. Her advice was to develop mechanisms and a team around you so you can focus on your particular expertise in your work, rather than thinking you have to do it all yourself.

Successful businesswomen with children are often asked, 'How do you do it all?' When she was asked this question in an interview, Emma Isaacs, Global CEO of Business Chicks, responded with an honest 'I don't and I couldn't do it all on my own'. She explained how the support team around her allowed her to run her global company while simultaneously taking on the other roles in her life, including as mother of four children.

> Creating a health team, tribe or community around us that supports our ability to be at our best is actually easier than you might think.

Today, if you need help with anything, most likely there is a service that can provide it. You would be amazed at what people get help with. From door-to-door ironing services to in-home chefs to virtual personal assistants, a myriad people and services are available to help you on your quest to switch off and create your own habitat for health.

The avalanche of available services can be overwhelming, confusing and expensive if you don't know exactly what you need or are looking for, so don't waste time, money and energy on trying to find a whole team of people at once. First decide on your highest priority, the big thing you need support with. What would have the biggest impact on your ability to create your habitat for health? Start there.

Use table 5 to help clarify your ideas (the first two rows contain examples). In the first column, write what area in your life you would like help with, then work out who it is you need. Fine-tune it a little further by asking yourself exactly what it is you need from them. Being specific from the outset can also save you time and money. Ask friends or go online to find the person/service who can help make your life so much easier, then fill in the last column in the table. Just ensure the person you are engaging is qualified and experienced and listens to you rather than just selling a product. After all, this is *your* team.

Table 5: my health team

What do I need help with?	Who can help me?	What do I need from them?	Where can I find them?
Getting fit	Local personal trainer	Accountability and exercise program	Really Fit Gym
House cleaning	Cleaner	To clean my house once a fortnight, top to bottom including bathrooms.	Super Clean Cleaners

When creating your health team keep in mind that its purpose is to help you be at your best. Your team may include health professionals to help you perform at your physical or mental best, professionals to help you play your A game at work, or organisers to help you stay on top of your responsibilities at home. No matter what you need, there are people who can help you. Some offer professional services you will need to pay for; others are friends and family only too happy to help if you ask them. You cannot know everything and have the solutions to all of your needs, and there is no shame in asking for help. Once you do, you'll wonder why you didn't do it sooner!

Get organised

One of the most important ways to make creating your habitat for health work is to get organised. For most of us it is one of those things we know we could do better, even if we don't like to admit it. We have all sent our kids to school in a dirty uniform or taken cookies from the lunchroom after forgetting to pack lunch, so there is no judgement here.

Being organised is really the key to ensuring the week flows smoothly. The reason busy people can do so much is that they are super organised. They are those people who plan meals, who have the clothes washed, paperwork filed and gym bag packed before they go to bed. The people who can do most are those who get themselves, and usually everyone else, organised.

The reason busy people can do so much is that they are super organised.

By being organised we cease to be reactive and become proactive. Being proactive means we are in control rather than just responding as things pop up. When we are organised our day flows better, and if we do forget something it isn't that big a deal.

Think back to the story of Leanne I shared in chapter 11. Through lack of planning, Leanne had set herself up for failure. To an outsider the solution was simple — get organised. If Leanne had looked after the simple things, like stocking up on groceries, preparing meals in advance, getting her workout clothes ready the night before and going to bed early, it would have worked. We could see that. By doing the little things she would have set herself up for success. Getting organised is easy to do and doesn't take a lot of time; in fact it saves time in the long run.

There are a few simple things you can do to get organised for success when creating a habitat for health. I want to be sure you heard that part: 'simple things'. Life is complicated enough without adding to it. If you want to get organised, make the process as simple as possible. I am often asked what is the best app for this. The simple answer is I have no idea. There are thousands of apps out there designed to help, from reminding us when to take medication to mapping the family's schedule. If you are taking too long finding or learning how to use an app, it is probably not time well spent. If you find one that works for you in the area where you most need help, then go ahead and use it. Getting organised needs to be as quick and simple as possible, so once you find your flow, stick with it. Here is a suggested flow you can adapt to your needs. It is a guide that has worked for many of my clients, and for me!

1. On Saturday, plan your meals for the coming week

Use a meal planning app or grab a pen and paper and write down what you will eat each night, from Sunday through to the following Saturday. If you get stuck for ideas, pick out some simple meals from a healthy recipe book. You can use your family favourites as a default or jump onto your favourite food site and make your selection. Remember to make them healthy and simple to prepare, particularly when you feel time poor. You don't have to take all of the load of making meals. Share it among the family by creating a cooking roster, ask your family their meal suggestions, and give yourself permission to have a night off every now and again. If you are the sole chef in the household, cook in batches so you can use a base in more than one meal during the week. It isn't cheating; it's being resourceful and using your time well!

2. Write down your shopping list

Be sure to include everything you'll need to make the meals in your plan, plus staples for breakfast, school lunches and healthy snacks you can take with you to work. The better prepared you are with food, the easier your week will be and the less likely you will be tempted by quick, unhealthy snacks. Creating your meal plan and shopping list should only take ten minutes, and the more you get into the hang of doing it the quicker it will become. Another great way to save time is to keep a list on the fridge and jot down items you run out of and need to replace. Remember, this is all about making your life easier. Most stores have shopping apps that can help you plan ahead. They are a great tool to keep you focused on the necessities and will even remind you to restock your staples, saving you time at your next shop.

3. Shop for groceries on the weekend

Shopping for food may feel like a waste of precious relaxation time, but the weekend is the best time to get the food you need for the week ahead. A general weekend shop saves time spent on those unnecessary daily trips to the shops during the week. If your weekends are fully taken up with racing between weekend sports and other events, another good time to shop is just before the weekend. Of course, if you love online shopping there are plenty of ways to have your groceries delivered to your door. Just remember, you'll really want a weekend delivery.

4. Spend an hour or two doing a cook-up

This is one of the hidden secrets of the super organised. With a refrigerator and pantry stacked full of food and a meal plan stuck on the fridge door, a big time saver is spending an hour or two on the weekend chopping up the veggies and meat for meals and bagging up healthy snacks for on-the-run snacks. Yes, you still have to make the meals on the day, but having at least some of the ingredients sliced and diced cuts preparation time during a busy week.

5. Plan your week on Sunday night

Again, I know it might feel as though you are cutting into your weekend, but in reality it is not very time-consuming and you'll become quicker each week. Take a look at your work week and your personal and family calendar. What do you have on? Do you need to arrange a babysitter for Friday night? Do you need to get to work early on Wednesday? Do you need to be home early to get to the board meeting? These can all add to the overwhelm of the week. Carefully planning for them in advance will help you start the week feeling prepared and in control so you are better able to respond to any unexpected developments.

6. Pack the night before

Have school bags, work bag, gym bag and/or after-school sport bags packed the previous evening. Mornings in any household are often chaotic, so reduce the stress by having everything packed and ready to go.

7. Set a routine

The key to being organised is to establish a routine. The simpler the routine we set up at home, the more likely everyone will follow it. Just like work systems, it provides a framework for getting things done. Using processes and routines doesn't make things boring; it streamlines our activities so we have more time to do other things—or, if we choose, to do nothing at all! Home routines might involve a jobs list kept on the fridge showing what the kids need to do after school, who unpacks the dishwasher and so on. The clearer the routines and expectations, the smoother your habitat for health will run.

8. Be realistic

When setting up your habitat for health, always remember to be realistic about what you can actually do in a day. Be clear about what you need to achieve by the end of the day or the week, and list the actions you need to take in the time available. Set a realistic target for each day, such as completing two priority tasks, then move on to the tasks of lower priority. Giving yourself a target of 40 tasks a day while only ever completing three is setting yourself up for disappointment and frustration. Getting organised is putting yourself in control, so set yourself targets that make you feel as though you are getting somewhere.

When you are organised you feel in control, so take the time to plan your week and you will have the energy to get through it *and* time to have some fun.

> Getting organised is putting yourself in control, so set yourself targets that make you feel as though you are getting somewhere.

When creating your habitat for health your picture is the foundation on which to build your success, and the people you surround yourself with enable and support you to be at your best. Being organised ties it all together so you can get on with what you need to do as well as what you want to do.

CHAPTER 13

Your time

The busier we become, the more we try to cram into our days and the less time we seem to have for ourselves. Too often we place our needs last, so when we finally collapse into bed we can only stare at the ceiling and long for some time on our own.

'I wish I had more time to myself' is a common lament. We conjure up images of freedom from the many demands on our time, spending hours at a spa or losing track of time while surfing the waves. Such imagining triggers a feeling of relaxation but is also freighted with guilt. The thought of taking time out for ourselves to be on our own and do whatever we choose is usually accompanied by a feeling that we are being selfish and worries about what it might mean for the family or for colleagues. So we put it off, discounting the possible benefits to ourselves or dismissing it as all too hard. Sadly, any request for me time tends to be viewed as evidence that we are not coping, and we don't like to be seen as not coping.

Carve out guilt-free me time

We usually take time out only when we really need to switch off, and when this happens we are often overtired, sick and in need of recuperation. Me time is complicated by negative associations with escapism, guilt and regret as well as overwhelm, stress and fatigue. All these negative connotations mean we tend to steer clear of it. Well, I am about to change your perception of the importance of me time, to persuade you that you should view it as vital for your health and wellbeing. Take this as permission to set aside some time for yourself!

Our need for time in which to do what we choose is increasingly urgent in an overconnected, overwhelmed and overstimulated world. As we are living faster, our life roles are changing. A woman may be a mum, a businesswoman, an executive, a volunteer and a coach. Women are juggling many roles within the home and in their professional lives, but it isn't just women who have experienced a shift in life roles.

In their personal and professional lives, men too are balancing different roles from what was expected 20, 30 or 50 years ago. Traditionally a man's role was as the breadwinner. He went to work early, worked hard all day, came home at the end of the day to a made meal, saw his family briefly if he was lucky, then went to bed, to follow the same routine the next day, and the next. Over the past 30 years we have seen men's roles shift from remote breadwinner to hands-on parent. Increasingly men are taking on the role of stay-at-home dad and primary caregiver while their partner goes to work.

The importance we ascribe to having time on our own also needs to change as we juggle multiple life roles, the demands these bring and the impact they have on our health and wellbeing.

Although we know work and life roles are changing, the information we are sharing on this topic has yet to catch up. Enter 'me time' in Google and you will see women lounging in day spas with cucumber slices over their eyes or walking contentedly on the beach—image after image of positive affirmations. At the time of writing, the first image of a man was of his feet curled up with a pair of women's feet in front of an open fireplace.

The importance of me time for men does not rate highly on discussion lists. In the focus groups conducted during research for this book, most women believed it was important for their partners to have time on their own. However, they also felt that when men did take time for themselves they did not experience the same amount of guilt as women do. The consensus among the women in these groups was that it is 'easier for men to switch off' and that they 'take it [me time] when they need it'.

The responses of the men in the groups were interesting. They understood the importance for their partner of taking time for themselves and said they encouraged her to do so. One shared his perspective on why men found it harder to make time for themselves: 'Men nowadays are expected to do so much more. We are expected to work, take on family roles, be fit, be involved with the kids' sports and activities. Sitting watching the footy or going for a surf is an important way for us to switch off from everything, but there seems so much to do nowadays that even these opportunities are becoming rarer'.

It isn't how much time we have, but rather what we do with it that matters.

At the British Psychological Society's Division of Occupational Psychology Annual Conference in Glasgow in 2015, Dr Almuth McDowall from the Birkbeck University of London, presented research into me time that drew on a mix of monthly diary entries and a questionnaire on work–life balance, family relationships, engagement at work and life satisfaction. The study found that the quantity of time spent in me time activities was not the critical factor in the experience of work–life balance, wellbeing and workplace engagement. What really counted was the quality of the time spent doing what we like. The study concluded that high-quality me time improved psychological wellbeing, relationships and productivity. It isn't how much time we have, but rather what we do with it that matters.

Taking time out for yourself has many physical and psychological benefits including:

- improved brain function
- better ability to process information
- improved concentration
- greater creativity
- improved memory function
- increased attention span
- improved productivity

- better decision-making skills

- space for self-discovery

- time for intuitive thinking

- reduced likelihood of burnout.

There are additional benefits for the family:

- The family probably needs a break from you too, so everyone wins.

- All the kids want to do is watch television anyway, so when you are not there they get to do what they want.

- Your partner will love the new you, as the stressed-out, cranky version is not much fun to be around.

Taking time for ourselves allows us to connect wholeheartedly with what it is we really love to do. We often settle for compromise to please others. We work with those around us to ensure everyone else is happy and their needs are met, even if our own are not. Spending time alone allows us to indulge ourselves in the things we love to do without having to consider anyone else's needs.

But is that what we really mean by taking time out? Through the focus groups conducted during the writing of this book I wanted to gain insights from a spectrum of people of different genders, employment backgrounds and cultures to find out what everyday people saw as me time, and if they were given the opportunity to take time for themselves what they would do with it. The results were interesting.

Across all groups there was a strong consensus that taking time out for yourself suggests selfishness, and that if you do so your partner should have a similar opportunity. If you go out shopping for the afternoon, surely your partner can watch the footy with his mates; if you take time to go have a coffee on your own in the morning, you feel like you should spend the afternoon with the kids.

So because me time often carries a sense of guilt and mutual obligation it is often not fully experienced and enjoyed. By associating it with self-indulgence, we fail to recognise the important part it plays in our being effective at work and at home. Even when we understand its importance for our health and happiness we continue to put the needs of others first.

Let's pause for a moment. Imagine you are given a whole day to do just as you please. No interruptions, no one else to think about, no appointments, no plans.

What will you do? Write it down now.

Ask 100 people this question and you would be surprised by the variations in responses, and even more surprised by how many would choose to spend their me time with someone else. Take a look at your 'me time' day. Is it all to be spent on your own, or have you chosen to have 'coffee with friends', 'dinner with your partner' or 'beach with the kids'? Me time implies time spent alone, but in reality it is about having the *ability to choose* how you use your time.

Rather than being a selfish luxury, me time is crucial to optimal health and wellbeing and to creating a habitat for health.

By seeing me time in terms of setting time aside for slowing down, re-energising and having fun, it can then be understood as less about selfishness and more about living the life you choose so you can be the very best version of yourself—an energetic, happy and fun person to be around. It's about taking time out from daily stressors, carving out space in which to think or relax. I want people to start to see me time as something that, rather than being a selfish luxury, is crucial to optimal health and wellbeing and to creating a habitat for health.

The many faces of me time

How you choose to use your time will vary widely depending on your needs and state of mind. Are you feeling exhausted? Do you need time on your own because you are feeling overwhelmed? Do you need a day's break from deadlines, a day of unscheduled play with your family? There are many versions of me time, from nourishing your body at a spa to going for a walk or a run to reading a book in bed. A creative activity such as painting, scrapbooking or drawing is another way to disconnect and get lost in your own space.

Me time is really about finding what it is that lights you up. It could be learning something new, hanging out with friends, going to the movies, spending time on social media, chatting with a neighbour, tinkering in the shed, hanging out with your kids, spending time with your partner, lying on the couch at night watching a movie that makes you laugh, or rerunning old home movies from when the kids were little. It could be something big and dramatic like 'I'm going to climb a mountain and find myself', but more likely it will be something as simple as a walk under the stars or just sitting on the verandah and watching the world go by. The list really is endless, but we need to grab the opportunities for these energy top-ups whenever and wherever they arise.

Me time is really about finding what it is that lights you up.

Those readers who still see these sorts of activities as an 'unproductive' use of time should think again. Certainly they are not directly measurable in terms of income generation, yet they are the foundation on which your best work is based, because after this time out you return to work revitalised and re-energised, with a spring in your step.

I am fortunate that every morning I get to drive along some of the most beautiful beaches in Australia, and before I reach the crest in the road that reveals the rolling waves and white sandy beaches I know if the surf is up. I know this by the number of cars parked along the roadside and, on a good day, the sea of surfers—men and women, boys and girls—gathered on the headland looking out over the ocean, soaking in the beauty and checking out the waves. Many of them, after their early-morning surf, will go home and don a business suit, drive to work and sit in an executive office all day before driving home, changing their suit for board shorts and a t-shirt and taking off again to check out the surf. Their days are bookended by an activity that helps release the pressures and overwhelm of the day. It is a valuable transition time that allows them to give their best to both their work and their family.

The activities we engage in at these transition points between home and work, and work and home impact on how we turn up in each environment. When we can use these times to switch off we are able to come home relaxed and go to work with focus.

One of the main reasons we don't prioritise me time is because we perceive ourselves as time poor. If this is you then try this simple way to mark out boundaries around your time, as well as creating a time you will look forward to every day.

I call it my 'personal happy hour'. Let's say you have one hour to spend just on you and your needs over a whole week. (If you really feel you don't have an hour a week, then we need to talk some more!) Could you block out ten minutes, six days a week, to meditate, watch television, focus on your breathing, go for a walk, have a cup of tea, listen to music? Remember, it is just 60 minutes out of the whole week. Can you give yourself that? I hope so.

Let's build on that. Once you have successfully carved out one hour a week for yourself, try for twice a week, then increase it until you are giving yourself one personal happy hour each and every day. Now that is a goal worth pursuing! Imagine the potential physical and psychological benefits you could reap from focusing on your own needs for one hour in every 24. Imagine, then schedule it in!

Whether you're wrangling toddlers, sleeplessly waiting for your teen to come home, caring for your ageing parents, or all of the above, everyone needs a break for sanity's sake. This means taking time each day to do something for yourself. Stuck for ideas? Here are 52 ways to switch off and have a little more me time.

52 ways to switch off

1. Go for a drive and explore somewhere new.

2. Colour in.

3. Explore Pinterest and Instagram for visual inspiration.

4. Go to the cafe on your own and don't tell anyone. (I've done this a few times myself!)

5. Go somewhere where you cannot connect to the internet. It is surprisingly liberating.

6. Go for a walk along the beach, in a park, anywhere there is sunlight and birds are chirping.

7. Go shopping when you don't have anything to buy.

8. Lie on your bed and stare at the ceiling. This will most likely end in a nap, so time well spent!

9. Have lunch in the park or anywhere outdoors.

10. Get your hair done.

11. Join a book club.

12. Go on a camping trip without your phone or tablet. I know, imagine!

13. Host a board games night. Invite a few friends over like the good old days, let laughter fill the house and have a great time.

14. Take your dog for a walk and don't take any photos or headphones—just walk your dog and enjoy the company.

15. Sit down to drink a cup of tea or coffee and actually taste it.

16. Read for pleasure.

17. Call a friend for a chat.

18. Walk over to a neighbour for a tea or coffee, or just to say hi.

19. On a Sunday afternoon turn up the music and cook your healthy meals for the week.

20. Have lunch in a cafe and watch people walk (or run) by.

21. Read a book to your kids in your bed earlier than bed-time without the usual stress and hurry.

22. Drive in the car with the music on...as loud as you want!

23. Close the office door and don't do any work (this one is so sneaky!).

24. Indulge in a physical maintenance review (in other words go to a day spa) or do a DIY at home and wax, pluck, shave and colour whatever needs it. You will feel fantastic afterwards.

25. Watch the reality show that has your partner rolling their eyes.

26. On your own, watch a show your partner hates, and change the channel as many times as you like (you know you love it!).

27. Have a cup of tea at night after everyone is asleep and the house is quiet.

28. Go out for lunch with a friend, no matter how long it takes.

29. Wake up half an hour earlier than everyone else.

30. Move more.

(continued)

52 ways to switch off (cont'd)

31. Go surfing, stand-up paddle boarding, kayaking or anything else you enjoy on the water.

32. Read one chapter of a book you've been hanging out to read.

33. Do something nice for the home, like buying new cushions or fixing that broken tile that has been bugging you.

34. Go out in the garden and pot a new plant.

35. Have a long soak in the bath.

36. Get a massage, a facial or anything on a day spa list. Guys, there is plenty on offer there for you too!

37. Take a nap during the day.

38. Go to a class that you've always wanted to do just for fun.

39. Take a long walk with a friend.

40. Have a date night with your partner...phones in your bags, not on the table.

41. Do yoga.

42. Meditate.

43. Collect shells on the beach (remember doing that as a child?).

44. Tinker in the shed on a project that you *want* to do, not have to do.

45. Wander through a plant nursery.

46. Flick through a magazine.

47. Look at old photos and reminisce about the good old days and laugh at the daggy clothes and hairstyles.

48. Go fishing.

49. Wash the car with your kids or partner and who knows, a water fight may ensue!

50. Light a candle, turn off the lights, put on some Barry White, grab a glass of wine and sit and talk with your partner, or watch a romantic comedy (or action thriller, if you prefer).

51. Work on an old car or restore a piece of furniture—rewarding and environmentally sound!

52. Simply do whatever you love to do, anything that makes you feel alive!

Quiet time

'Me time' isn't the only use of time that is good for our health. The concept of quiet time has been adopted by daycare and preschool centres for years and has been a part of the parenting toolkit for generations. Many cultures have embraced the afternoon siesta, where after a morning of hard work businesses close for a long meal and a couple of hours' rest. The siesta has been practised across the Mediterranean and southern Europe for many generations as a way to rest and re-energise in the heat of the afternoon. Unfortunately western cultures generally have not taken up the practice, in spite of medical evidence supporting it. Against the natural energy cycles of the body, workers across the western world continue to push through their day with diminished energy and focus. Bring on the siesta, I say!

Yet we have accepted the importance of quiet time for our children. After lunch and a little outside active play, daycare centres roll out mattresses so little children can curl up for an hour or two of rest mid afternoon. With quiet time a part of their daily schedule, children have the energy to carry them through an active afternoon of painting, running, climbing, listening, learning and exploring.

For many parents, afternoon quiet time during the school holidays is a saviour. After a hectic morning and lunch, the television is switched on for an afternoon movie, tablets are brought out or children are sent to their bedroom for reading or quiet play. Parents understand that without quiet time the children will become unbearable by dinner, so quiet time is valuable for everyone, especially parents. Quiet time provides solace in a hectic day.

Have you ever been driving along in your car with the radio on while having a conversation? After a time you realise you are not really paying attention to either; all you can hear is the blending of voices with the blur of the radio. Once you turn off the radio you can pay more attention to the person speaking. The persistent background noise divides your attention so you are not effectively tuning into anything. This can be the result of constant activity and persistent stimulation.

Quiet time allows us to turn down the noise, to rest and repair, to notice, to take time out...to switch off. Additionally, it gives us the opportunity to clear our mind and connect with how we are feeling in that moment. I remember as a new mum being given the advice that when my baby slept so should I, so I could also be rested. At the time I scoffed at this idea (even though I'd heard it many times), because this was my opportunity to get all my chores done. There was just no time to rest. This meant that the only time I ever rested was when I was exhausted. Looking back, I wish I had listened to the wisdom of people who had lived in a time that wasn't so frantic. Whether I rested or not, the chores were always there and never seemed to be completed. If I had my time again I would snatch up with both hands every opportunity to take a nap!

Quiet time allows us to turn down the noise,
to rest and repair, to notice, to take
time out...to switch off.

One benefit of quiet time (although we might not like to admit it) is that it allows us to switch off from others. As harsh as it may sound, being around other people all the time can be exhausting. As we discussed earlier in the book, being connected to people 24/7 leaves little time to focus on ourselves, our own needs and those of the people who matter most to us. Disconnecting gives us the opportunity to decompress in the calm of our own space, to focus on our own energy rather than the mixed and often overwhelming energy of everyone else in our lives.

You may feel compelled to take some quiet time as a reaction to feeling overconnected, overwhelmed or overstimulated. A better option is to use it as a preventive tool, scheduling it in, preferably in the afternoon and particularly on weekends. Use this time for yourself and your family, so everyone has a chance to switch off. Look for technology-free activities, as staying connected can counteract the benefits of taking time out in the first place.

If you find carving out quiet time challenging, try starting small, even if it is only five minutes a day. As discussed in earlier chapters, practising meditation or breathing exercises or journaling are all great ways to spend quiet time. In time you will find these practices come more naturally, and although the time will pass quicker the benefits will also be achieved more quickly.

Become aware of others' needs for quiet time. When your children take themselves off to their room to read a book at the end of the day they are often self-regulating, meaning they are creating their own opportunity to decompress, find calm and switch off.

A research paper published in *Frontiers in Psychology* explored the benefits and differences of unstructured versus structured activity time for children and how both impacted on complex cognitive abilities such as switching between tasks, resisting impulses and attention. The research found that children who spent more time in unstructured activities, such as playing alone or with friends, singing or bike riding, performed better in all areas compared with those who undertook more structured activities, such as sports practice, piano lessons or homework.

By scheduling unstructured quiet time into our day we are providing ourselves with opportunities to switch off mentally and physically and in doing so hit the reset button, giving us the energy to take us through the rest of the day. Creating even a 10- to 15-minute window of quiet time will have personal, health and productivity benefits.

Some great quiet time activities (for you and your family)

- Read a book.

- Watch a slow movie (not the hyped-up, fast-paced kind that only stimulate viewers further).

- Undertake an activity you find relaxing, such as sewing, making jewellery or tinkering in the shed.

- Paint, draw or colour in.

- Children (or even adults!) can play in their room with Lego or build model planes.

Any activity that helps you to calm down and focus on something you enjoy is good for quiet time. This is not 'productive time'; it is down time, a chance to chill out.

CHAPTER 14

To be at your best

The reason for creating a habitat for health is to help you be at your best, with the energy and vitality to do the things in life you need and want to do. Your body is the vehicle that carries you through life and everything you do. Once it breaks down and stops functioning as it should, you cease to be available to others. When you are too busy your health is often the first thing you will de-prioritise while you focus on what needs to be done at home and at work. It is important to listen and take notice of what your body needs to nourish itself, and to tap into the people who can help you.

Get physical

Physical fitness is a vital component of our health. We put our body under pressure, demanding that it sustain us through some pretty heavy punishment. In return, too many of us are not giving our bodies the love and attention or the fuel they need and deserve.

It is important to listen and take notice of what your body needs to nourish itself, and to tap into the people who can help you.

We all know the importance of being physically fit. I'm not talking about workout fitness to make us musclebound or ripped. I am talking about being well, having the energy, the stamina and the strength to carry us comfortably through the day.

Is your body allowing you to move through your day with gusto? Do you have the mental focus to do the work you need to? Are you giving it the fuel it needs and the rest it deserves?

Through the media we are constantly fed images of what good health should look like, but we are starting to realise these images do not necessarily match the reality of human physiology. There are endless sources of information available to us on our nutritional needs and how we should train, use and care for our bodies, and herein lies the challenge: how can we know what is right for us when creating our habitat for health? It seems like every day a new research paper is released staking out what science has now proved to be best for our health. I am a health professional and even I find it confusing. Creating your habitat for health comes down to a very important point: it is *your* habitat. You have to create the environment that will help you be at your best. So it is important that the way you interpret the mass of health information is right for you, but how do you know?

The best place to start is to take what you learned through the phases of switching off. You will have noticed how your body feels when you are not at your best. Once you have honestly determined how you are feeling and what your body may be lacking, tap into your health team and listen to their advice, but also try new things—test, research, ask and listen. When you feel you have educated yourself sufficiently and are ready to make the physical changes, make the decision that will allow you to be at your best, then just start. Start moving more, eating better, sleeping longer and slowing down ...

Whatever your physical health right now, sit with it, acknowledge it and then do something about it. Be in control of your health before your body tells you what it needs. You can't afford for illness or injury to take control, so if you feel you need help with getting started or staying on track, connect with people who can educate you, motivate you and support you on your health journey.

Look beyond the walls

Heading outdoors has many physiological benefits. One of the most significant is that it encourages us to switch off from the overstimulation of a stressful day, freeing us from our often confined, busy workplace. When I have had a long day indoors I need to take myself outside and get some fresh air before the day is done. While writing this book I would deliberately offset a long stretch at the computer with a walk to the beach or a ride to the local cafe or a basketball match with the kids after they got home from school. My body and my mind needed that time outdoors to 'clear my head'. Creating this space means seeing our health environment as larger than our workplace or home, and broadening our options and inspiration when creating our habitat for health.

In an article in *Psychology Today* titled 'Creating Space: How well does your surrounding environment draw out your creative potential?', Yosef Brody describes a central ambivalence in his life. Although he loves living in the city, he also longs to experience nature and the outdoors. 'Beyond an intense desire to be near trees and water, I get overwhelmed by a strange need to look towards the horizon.' He calls his condition 'cyburbanitis'. His city overwhelm and constant connection through technology, he finds, has an effect on his ability to focus and be creative: 'my vision, taken up by walls and buildings everywhere, becomes blocked and constrained'.

Through the open expansiveness of the outdoors we can regain perspective. To see beyond the confines of our office, our shop, our home, to look to the horizon, opens our field of view to take in the broadness of nature and everything it hold for us. No longer trapped in our micro world we reconnect with the enormous potential of the world around us.

Cheryl Strayed's memoir *Wild* beautifully depicts the profound impact the outdoors can have on the way we view our world; a movie adaptation was released in 2015. After the death of her mother (played by Laura Dern) and the breakdown of her marriage, Cheryl (Reese Witherspoon) plunged into a spiral of self-destructive behaviour that saw her life fall apart around her. After hitting rock bottom, she knew she had to change her life. She had the idea that she needed to reconnect with who she was and where she was heading. With no outdoors experience, Cheryl sets out alone to hike the Pacific Crest Trail, a tough long-distance trail across three American states. Through the challenges she meets and the beauty and demands she encounters on her journey she is ultimately able to find a kind of peace and perspective in her life.

You don't need to take on a months-long mountain hike to reach beyond your immediate environment. Broadening your perspective can be as simple as lifting your eyes from your screen to look out the window towards the distance. Doing so allows you to disconnect from the here and now and let your mind wander. It's a simple way to flick the switch as needed throughout your day without ever leaving your desk. You can then quickly return to the task at hand with renewed focus.

Broadening your perspective can be as simple as lifting your eyes from your screen to look out the window towards the distance.

Ensure that your habitat for health includes the outdoors. Your habitat, after all, is the environment you live in. You don't need to wait until the weekend or hold off until your next holiday to disconnect from work.

Create your habitat for health

Your habitat for health must be integrated into all areas of your life, including your work day. Look for opportunities throughout the week to get outdoors and take in your surroundings. Here are some more ideas to help you:

- Eat breakfast on the verandah. Spending time outdoors, breathing fresh air and looking out at your surroundings, is a great way to start your day.

- Go outside for other meal breaks too.

- Look out to the horizon through your office window when on the phone or during extended periods at your desk.

- Use an outdoor image as your screen saver, especially one that inspires you or evokes happy memories. You will feel like you are being transported to that place just by looking at the image.

- At the end of the work day, instead of switching on the television and getting straight into the night-time routine, take the family or yourself for a walk or a bike ride. Play in the backyard, drive to the local park or do some gardening (even if it is limited to a rooftop or patio garden). Rather than bouncing from one hectic environment to another, give yourself a natural break.

- Once all the family is in bed go sit outside and look up at the stars. Seriously, when was the last time you really took in the night sky? We have our heads down so much we forget to look up. It sounds a little out there, but looking up will also open your airways and you'll feel immediately calmer as you marvel at the beauty of the stars, the sounds of the night and the feel of the cool fresh air on your skin. Everyone has time to look up once in a while.

Get creative

We have long understood the importance of creativity—as a way to express ourselves and assist communication and as an outlet for mental anguish associated with trauma and stress. While we often associate it with leisure pursuits or hobbies, many professions, such as graphic design, fashion and marketing, draw directly on creativity. Health professionals recognise creativity as an important emotional and expressive outlet and helps to develop play skills in children.

As a paediatric occupational therapist I once worked with a young boy, Ryan, who had been diagnosed with Autism Spectrum Disorder. Ryan was unable to articulate his feelings verbally and had significant challenges with social relationships, social rules and appropriate behaviours. He was a beautiful young boy with an extremely kind soul. Following the diagnosis it was an emotional time for the family. It was an overwhelming period for young Ryan, who was subjected to numerous tests, with different adults asking him questions and putting him through routines that he found challenging. His family hoped I could assist him with his sensory regulatory behaviours and help him with his gross and fine motor skill development.

Ryan was fortunate to have a team of very committed, caring and skilled therapists including speech pathologists and paediatricians working with him. During one session I noticed he wanted to engage with me but had difficulty doing so. Although he was not able to communicate with me verbally, I was convinced he knew exactly what I was saying when I spoke.

In my therapy rooms I had a wall that was covered with an old-style blackboard. Ryan picked up a piece of chalk and sat at the board and started to make marks on it. At first I couldn't make out what he was drawing, so I too grabbed a piece of chalk and sat alongside him and started to draw my own picture. After a little while of looking back and forth between his drawing and mine, Ryan's drawing started to make sense to me. I could see the form of a young boy, a tree and some swings. With no words exchanged I took my chalk and just near his tree I drew the shape of a bird. I knew this was a little risky as Ryan liked being in his own space. I then returned to drawing my little girl in a park. A few moments later he reached over and next to my little girl he drew what resembled a flower. I'll share with you that I had to struggle hard to hold back my tears. I was overcome with emotion as I looked towards Ryan and on his gorgeous tanned face was the hint of a smile, and although he wasn't looking at me I caught a cheeky glint in his eyes I had never seen before.

We had made a connection, not through words but through creativity. This moment was the start of the visual banter between us. Ryan allowed me to enter his space through the imagery we created. By the end of a few sessions Ryan was creating images that showed me the pain and loneliness he was feeling, but equally a joy and wonder in nature that I would never have come to know through words.

I often reflect on this experience, and wonder at what point in our lives we stop placing importance on our creativity. Is it when life becomes too busy? Is it when our social life takes priority? Or is it when we no longer consider creativity as playing a 'productive' role in our work, unless we are in the 'creative industries'? Whatever the reason, we need to bring creativity back into our lives for all the same reasons that we encourage it in kids—as an emotional outlet, as a channel for our imagination, as a way to calm ourselves and to dream. It can be really hard to talk about our feelings, especially when we don't know how or can't find the words to express what we feel. Art bridges the gap between emotion and expression by encouraging avenues other than words through which to express ourselves.

We need to bring creativity back into our lives for all the same reasons that we encourage it in kids—as an emotional outlet, as a channel for our imagination, as a way to calm ourselves and to dream.

It is vitally important that we have a tool that enables us to switch off from the pressures of life and reconnects us to the joy that creativity brings.

Human beings are naturally creative and as we become more overwhelmed, more outcome focused and more pressured to achieve, the importance of bringing creativity into our professional work is increasingly recognised. It is not uncommon now to see sticky notes, textas and butcher paper covering the tables in planning meetings and training rooms. Doodling on a notepad during a meeting is also no longer frowned on. We are becoming more aware that when given every opportunity to be creative, people are more innovative, think outside the box and find solutions that are often not seen through prescriptive processes.

Taking just half an hour out of your week to do something creative—whether drawing, painting or singing a song—will benefit your health.

So step back from the overwhelm and reconnect with your inner creativity. You will think more clearly, gain new perspectives on the world and have fun in the process.

There are many ways, even when under time pressure, to tap into your creativity. Here are a few ideas to try:

Unlock ideas through drawing or writing

Research has been conducted across many industries to determine the best starter for creativity. The simplest way to start any process or idea generation is to grab a pencil and paper and start drawing or writing. What will be unlocked through drawing or writing may surprise you. When it comes to creativity there is no right or wrong way or style. Sometimes the worst mistakes turn into the best ideas.

Take a break

In 2009 designer Stefan Sagmeister presented a talk at TED Global that has since been viewed more than 2.5 million times. Stefan shared how every seven years he closes his New York design studio to take a year-long sabbatical so he can refresh his creativity. He explains it is often during this 'time off' that he comes up with his best ideas, as he uses his time to work on projects that inspire him, teach him a new skill or allow him to switch off.

Work on a different project

Stationery company 3M understand the value of tapping into their staff's creativity. They encourage their staff to use 15 per cent of their work time on developing new ideas. Staff are able to work on a project they normally wouldn't be involved in or that hasn't been developed yet. The Post-it note has been just one payoff from this initiative (and we have all used a few of those in our time!).

Go to the local market

Markets and farmers' markets are popping up everywhere as a way for locals and tourists to support local artisans and suppliers by buying their handmade wares and home-grown produce. Take a morning to wander around the stalls and be inspired by the skills on display, and take some of the ideas home with you. Perhaps you'll decide to grow a veggie garden, or maybe the smell of handmade soap will spark your passion for creating gifts again.

Check out Pinterest and Etsy for inspiration

Spend some time on these sites and you will find all sorts of ideas. Whether you want to carve people-shaped ice-blocks, create the ultimate man-cave or plan the perfect birthday party, creative inspiration is at your fingertips.

Take time to daydream

We have talked about the importance of time on your own; now give yourself permission to daydream! Creativity is sparked through imaginative thought. Bill Gates, the founder of Microsoft and one of the most financially successful people in the world, takes twice-yearly 'think weeks', during which he removes himself to a secluded retreat for the purpose of daydreaming, thinking about and planning his next six months. It is through this thinking time that he comes up with his best ideas. If you don't have a secluded retreat to hive off to twice a year, then take ten minutes each week or even each day to stare out the window and dream up your next adventure, your next project or your next idea. So your brilliance is not lost, make sure you write your ideas down somewhere. Maybe you just thought up the next billion-dollar idea.

Have fun

When creating your habitat for health you need to stay attuned to why you are doing it in the first place. Is it to gain better health, to create more energy, to feel less distracted? Whatever your reason, creating a habitat for health needs to be fun and meaningful or you won't stick with it.

Working with children, I was constantly reminded of the innate sense of fun, lightheartedness and joy they possess. Children can make fun out of anything and have fun with anyone. On one occasion my last appointment for the day was with Luke, a young boy of eight. It had been a long day and I was ready to switch off and go home. I was feeling flat, a little stressed, and my brain was starting to power down. Luke came in and we started the session. To his credit he was on task and willing to do what I asked. About ten minutes into the session he looked up and said, 'What's wrong with you?' I paused, a little aghast at his frankness, and replied with a stern 'Excuse me?' He said, 'You just seem a little boring today'. After another shocked pause I couldn't help but smile, realising he was absolutely right ... I was being boring! Out of the honest mouth of a child, I was brought back to Earth with a thud. Children see the world through the lens of fun. If it isn't fun, they don't want to do it. Both process and outcome have to be fun, and it has to have a point (think of the five-year-old asking, Why? Why? Why?).

As adults we too want a life filled with fun, happiness and joy. Just look at the wave of new books being published about finding happiness and joy and even how to bring laughter back into our lives through laughter workshops. On the whole children are pretty carefree (or they should be), but as adults we find ourselves becoming ever more serious as we wrestle with work, family and financial responsibilities. Life can be stressful and at times it is no fun at all. Despite wanting fun in our lives, we find it hard to let the seriousness go; we are too bogged down to have a laugh.

A young intern who was working with us and witnessing the franticness that comes with meeting a tight deadline looked at me and declared fervently, 'I never want to grow up—it's too stressful!' For a young person, serious, stressed-out adults would look frightening, and not very inspirational.

There comes a time in our lives when grownup responsibility starts to take over, when being serious starts to overshadow having fun, which becomes something we do only after work or when we are on holiday. Much of the evidence indicates that people who lead lives filled with laughter, social connectedness and adventure are happier, feel more fulfilled and live without regret.

In the pursuit of creating a habitat for health that involves fun, my friends and I decided to put these studies to the test. Could we be grownups with responsibilities, work pressures, deadlines and children and still have fun? Our list of activities included a Pink concert (I thought I was 20 again!), dinner out at a funky restaurant, a game of snooker at the local pub, a Sunday afternoon barbecue and drinks, and breakfast the next morning. This may not sound like the wildest program, but let's just say we can still rock like it was 1999. We laughed about it for months afterwards. We had so much fun not because of what we did, but because we made the time to get together with the purpose and the intention of having fun. We might be older, and we might talk a lot about work and kids, but given half a chance we could still boogie (okay, so I just showed my age there; for millennials, that's a funky word for dance), we could still be a little mischievous and we could certainly let our hair down.

> People who lead lives filled with laughter, social connectedness and adventure are happier, feel more fulfilled and live without regret.

Creating your habitat for health has to be done with lightness, with joy, and if it doesn't give you sore cheeks, a jiggling belly and awesome memories then is it really worth it?

Work can also be fun — it should be fun. Many business owners started out purely because they wanted to work with their passion. They loved what they did, they turned up at work with a spring in their step and joy in their work. That's the fun part about being in business: you are doing something you love that puts a fire in your belly. Even when you've had two hours of sleep and are working an 80-hour week, you know the effort is worth it; you are having fun. But soon the serious side of business — compliance, tax, administration — starts to take over, and the fun flame starts to burn down. We begin to fall out of love for our work.

But don't fear, it's never too late to rekindle the fun flame. Watch a group of middle-aged men at a bucks weekend or a group of ladies letting their hair down at a long lunch. If we give ourselves permission and create the time to have fun, we'll find the fun is still inside. And your gender doesn't matter either; men and women alike are crying out for the time and energy to do the things they love and have a good laugh. Scheduling fun doesn't sound very much fun but it is a good place to start if you are stuck in your diary. Book in a concert, a dinner, a barbecue or a trip to the movies so you can have fun with people who make you laugh. If you don't have anyone in your life who makes you laugh, it might be time to look at the people you surround yourself with.

No job is so serious that you can't bring light and laughter into the work, as demonstrated by my friend the motivational speaker Robi Mack, who for ten years was known as Dr Have-A-Chat, a clown doctor at the Sydney Children's Hospital. It was Robi's role, her job and her purpose to bring happiness and joy to children living with a terminal illness. During a child's and a family's darkest times clown doctors inject hope and lightness through the gift of fun and laughter. 'Working with children with significant illnesses gives you a perspective on life that you typically would not get,' Robi shared with me. 'I saw my time as a clown doctor as a gift from the children; it was my heart job. I learned throughout this time that when you put your concerns and worries aside, you can connect with people and positively impact on their lives'.

There is no job where lightness and laughter cannot be embraced. Whether it is an integral part of the job or a way of coping with the stressors, injecting fun and laughter into your job will allow you to take control of how you approach each day.

Inject fun into your life

If you have forgotten how to have fun, here are a few simple ways to inject fun back into your life:

- Stop whatever you are doing for 30 minutes to wrestle with the kids, without your phone in hand. Unless you are waiting on a call from the prime minister for your input on the next election, or Oprah wants to meet with you personally to hear your views on life, then my guess is any call can wait. Play with your kids, because they won't be kids forever.

- Ask a group of your friends over for an impromptu barbecue where everyone brings a plate of food (like the good old days before *MasterChef* made us all feel like we need to be perfect hosts) and have a relaxing, fun afternoon of backyard cricket, bocce or conversation.

- Check out the local paper to see what bands are coming to a location near you. If you haven't noticed, a lot of eighties and nineties favourites are making comebacks, and they are playing everywhere. You never know which childhood idol will be playing at your local.

- Stop checking Facebook at the dinner table to find out what everyone else is doing with their lives; switch off and enjoy yours. Listen to the stories your children are sharing from their school day. These conversations are often hilarious and insightful.

(continued)

Inject fun into your life (*cont'd*)

- Stop racing to work, racing from work to the gym and back again, racing to swimming, racing home for dinner, rushing to the computer to check your work emails (that can wait until 7 am when you are back at work), and after distracted conversation with your partner falling into bed and sleep because you are so exhausted. Slow down, look up, breathe and smile. Life is good.

- With a neighbour, a friend, your partner or a group consisting of some or all of the above head down to the local tennis court for a hit of tennis. Can't play? Even better! Watching you run across a tennis court grunting and groaning will add to everyone's fun. One hour every now and again will be great for your body, and imagine the abdominal workout from the laughs.

In creating your habitat for health you are setting up an environment to help you be the very best version of yourself you can be. With a clear understanding of what your picture of health is, you can make sound decisions that support your health and wellbeing. Whether you are seeking to carve out more time for yourself, to find calm in the frantic storm of your life or to bring back your creative edge, your habitat for health is key to ensuring your success. Be clear about what you want, tap into the people around you and create daily habits that allow you to flick the switch when you need to.

To help create your habitat for health, take some time to work through the following checklist. Before you know it, you will be living and breathing the best version of you.

- ☐ Create your ideal habitat for health, complete with pictures.

- ☐ Establish your health team.

- ☐ Get yourself organised.

- ☐ Carve out guilt-free 'me time'.

- ☐ Get active.

- ☐ Look beyond your immediate surroundings and get outdoors.

- ☐ Get creative.

And above all else, don't forget to have fun!

FINAL MESSAGE

This book has introduced you to more than 250 ways to switch off. You have learned about the importance of taking the time to slow down and focus on your health and wellbeing. I hope you now feel you have the tools and the strategies to help you regain control in your life.

There may still be times when it seems like if you add one more thing to your schedule you will tip over the edge, and there will be times when you feel completely calm and in control. Wherever you find yourself in life, know you can use this book as a reference point, a source of ideas, a reminder that everything you need in life is already here for you.

In a world that continues to accelerate, take heart in knowing that you do not have to run faster to keep up. To thrive, you have to embrace the opportunities in front of you, stay focused on the here and now, and take the time to look around you, knowing that the universe will always supply you with what you need, if you just slow down long enough to notice.

Now, it's in your hands.

Angela

INDEX

Keep updated with information and inspiration

Follow Angela on:

Twitter: @angelockwood
Facebook: Angela Lockwood
Instagram: @angelalockwood_
Pinterest: Angela Lockwood
LinkedIn: Angela Lockwood

www.angelalockwood.com.au